THE WORLD'S MOST

EXTRAORDINARY YACHTS

By Jill Bobrow & Dana Jinkins

JILL BOBROW
&
DANA JINKINS

Concepts Publishing

THE WORLD'S MOST
EXTRAORDINARY YACHTS

For Bill and Kenny

Second Edition

Library of Congress Cataloging-in-Publication Data

Bobrow, Jill, 1951-
   The world's most extraordinary yachts.

   1. Yachts and yachting.   I. Jinkins, Dana,
1950-   . II. Title.
VM331.B67   1986   623.8'233   86-17166
ISBN 0-393-03314-7

ISBN 0-393-03314-7: U.S. Edition
ISBN 0-9611712-1-9: U.K. Edition

Acknowledgements

Author/Publisher . . . . Jill Bobrow
Photographer/Creative Director . . . . .Dana Jinkins
Associate Editor . . . . .William Stedman
Art Director/Associate Designer . . . . .Elizabeth Prinz
Accommodation Plan Illustrators . . . . .Marcia Johnson
    James Eastland, Martha Donovan
Design Consultant . . . . .Randell Pearson
Copy Editor . . . . Jeremy Townsend
Communications . . . . Kenneth Mitchnick
Designer Notes . . . . .Joe Artese,
    Jon Bannenberg, Gertrude Denison, Terence Disdale,
    Susan Puleo, Roy Sklarin, Pierre Tanter, Giorgio Vafiadis
Final pages painting of Portofino . . . . .Karla Joy Bove

Printing. . .Dai Nippon Printing Company Ltd., Tokyo, Japan.
Typography. . .Blue Pen Typografix, New York.

Concepts Publishing
RR#1, Box 500,
Moretown, Vt. 05660

Distributed in the U.S. & Canada by: W. W. Norton &
Company, Inc. 500 Fifth Avenue, New York, N.Y. 10110

Distributed in Great Britain by Collectors' Books
Bradley Lodge, Kemble, Cirencester, Glos. GL76AD England

We would like to express our gratitude to all of the yacht owners, captains and crew, who welcomed us aboard, answered all of our questions, and allowed us to take photographs. We would also like to thank several others who assisted us in a variety of ways: B. Martin Pedersen, Arna Pedersen, James Mairs, George Nicholson, Kimio Honda, Christian and Mary Rose Brann, Melanie Jones, Sandra Frazier, Randi Jinkins, Bonnie O'Boyle, Jenny Tudor Miles, George Sustendal, Alessandro Vitelli, Mark Hilpern, Mike Ringdahl, John Warren, Don Kenniston, John Schneberger, Erik Pascoli, Jim Castle, Alexis Witzig-Vejarana, Gerhard and Simonetta Killian, Bruno Cantilupi, Fabio Perini, Maurizio Pocai, Richard Taylor, Carlo Traglio, John Barden, Fred Dovaston, Claire Oppenheim, and Lamia Khashoggi. The majority of photographs were taken by Dana Jinkins. Those not taken by her are individually accredited and greatly appreciated. We would like to give special thanks to the photographers pictured below.

Dana Jinkins is a photographer and artistic director for Concepts Publishing. She designed this book and her photographs comprise most of this volume. When she's not working on a book project, she designs boat brochures and does freelance photography. Dana has an extensive photographic bank of yacht and travel photography.

Mike Meade, a Canadian, has lived and worked as a photographer on the French Riviera for fifteen years. He has a well-founded reputation in every aspect of yacht photography. His small chase boat *Flash* is a familiar sight along the French coastline. His latest tool, a Weedhopper microlight aircraft (on floats) is an ideal platform for underway aerial photography during the summer months.

Tony Morgan, born in 1909 in France, is a journalist and a photographer who has traveled extensively with his work. He now lives in Monaco, and maintains a large archive of marine photographs which includes over four hundred yachts. He enjoys his work and has no plans of retiring in the near future.

Philip Harrill, an American, operates two yacht related businesses with his wife: an interior design business and a brochure business. He photographs yachts of all kinds and his company, The Brochure People, is located in Ft. Lauderdale, Florida.

Contents

Key to boat specifications:

LOA: Length overall
LOD: Length on deck
LWL: Length waterline
Draft: Maximum depth from the waterline to the keel
Beam: Maximum width
Year: Year built
Hull: The boat's construction
CBU: Centerboard Up
CBD: Centerboard Down

The view of Villefranche from the coast road between Monaco and Nice, is breathtaking.

The harbor at St. Tropez is a popular spot among yachts during the summer season.

Le Grazie in the province of La Spezia is an idyllic harbor town in Liguria on the coast of Italy. Several beautiful yachts are docked here, tucked away from the large marinas. It is here that the lovely schooner Orion is based.

Megayachts have been a growing trend in the last few years. In researching this book, Dana and I have traveled to the top yards in Europe and the States. Even to Japan, where the supertankers are being replaced by private yachts in the 4 to 20 million dollar range. Yacht Builders have waiting lists of two to three years, some even longer, as the market for yachts over 100 feet grows amazingly strong.

What is causing this surge in megayacht building? George Nicholson, international yacht broker, says that satellite communications equipment, more than anything else, has made these impractical yachts practical. Most owners of megayachts are businessmen who cannot afford to be out of touch for very long. Thus, with instant private and secure communications via satellite and, of course, the convenience of telex machines, yachting has become a more convenient as well as attractive way of life for the successful entrepreneur. Each megayacht now being built is a world unto itself.

The concept of having your own world is appealing in many ways. A theory that has been postulated is that the trend toward building megayachts comes from the alleged fear of the upcoming nuclear holocaust and/or the triumph of Communism in Western Europe. Therefore, capitalists are buying yachts which have incredible transoceanic range, to provide islands of safety to which they can retreat.

Dana and I have always been fascinated by boats and the notion of transporting your own home anywhere in the world. In 1982, we published our first book, *Classic Yacht Interiors*. At that time we shared a prediliction for sailboats, particularly older, wooden vessels that had been lovingly restored. We also concentrated on the East Coast and the Caribbean. We are into our third printing of that book and have been gratified to find it on coffee tables and in book shelves around the world.

At first we resisted the notion of a volume II, a "son of" yacht book, as being repetitious. But Jim Mairs, vice president of W. W. Norton & Company who distributes our books, urged us to produce a book on classic motor yachts. Jeff Hammond, publisher of *Power and Motor Yacht* magazine wanted us to help out with the August issue covering the annual P&MY 100—the world's top yachts. We decided not to limit ourselves to the classic or old. We also decided to please friends and fans of our first book by including some truly incredible sailboats, along with the motor yachts.

The number of magnificent vessels in the world made our task of choosing which boats to include a tremendously difficult one. Our criteria for including the yachts were that they must be custom, unique, outrageous, and, of course, extraordinary. Yet even with such stiff standards to follow, we were forced, for the sake of space, to exclude many boats which fit the bill.

Many people have asked us how we went about discovering these yachts, and how we were able to obtain permission to photograph the interiors. First of all, word of mouth has always been most helpful. "Did you see that gigantic blue yacht *Carintha* at its own dock in Cannes?" someone will ask, or "Have you ever been aboard Niarchos's yacht *Atlantis II*?" and "What about the three-masted schooner that was just built in Mallorca?" Through the guidance (and gossip) of other yacht enthusiasts, we would discover more and more incredible boats. But discovery was only half the battle, for we were still left with the difficult assignment of gaining permission from the captains to board the vessel and photograph it for publication. Megayacht owners tend to cherish their privacy, and the captains see to it that that privacy is respected. We are, however, very determined, and when a boat caught our attention, we didn't balk.

We actually began this book in 1983 by arranging to shoot the interior (or lack of it) of America's Cup winner *Australia II*. That same time in Newport, R.I. we arranged to photograph M/Y *Kalizma* because she used to belong to Elizabeth Taylor and Richard Burton. For a short while we got side-tracked and worked in spurts and on inspiration, like when we discovered that the newly launched megasloop *Whitefin* was racing the equally impressive *Whitehawk* at the Opera House Cup race in Nantucket. We knew we had to be there.

To truly begin, however, we knew that the Mediterranean was the place for us to go. You can't exactly telephone to find out where a yacht is going to be at any given time, since their owners plans are usually capricious. We began walking the docks of Monte Carlo, passing the Rolls-Royces and bodyguards and literally knocking on the hulls of yachts carrying our "green book," *Classic Yacht Interiors*, under our arms as a sort of calling card. At *Atlantis II* we couldn't get past the third aft deck hand. On another half dozen swank Cantieri de Pisa motor yachts with Arab letters on the transom, we were waved off—sorry but security, you know. But if we had the opportunity to leave our book on board for the owner to peruse, we then had much better luck, especially after we explained that our book was about boats, not people.

Our list of prospective yachts, as lengthy as it was, did have priorities. First of all, we wanted to shoot the yacht *Nabila*. I was able to speak to the owner's wife, Mrs. Khashoggi, via satellite telephone while she was onboard *Nabila*, and she told us to come to Naples in the next two days to photograph the yacht. We flew to Rome and called the Khashoggi's secretary in Cannes. Apparently the yacht was having some repairs done and it was not an appropriate time to photograph her since many of the valuables would be locked up. So when can we do the job? we asked. Oh, we'll call you. Dana and I didn't exactly have a plan of where we would be next; it all depended on where the subjects were, so I arranged to call the office in Cannes frequently. I felt like a character in a Woody Allen movie who calls to leave a new number at every stop: "Hello, this is Jill Bobrow, today we are in Viareggio. Tomorrow we'll be in La Spezia. We don't have a hotel number in Portofino…yet. We'll call back when we find a place." So as not to waste time

Nice, because of the airport, is the hub of the Cote d'Azur. From here vacationers travel both east and west to private homes, resorts, and yachts.

Porto Cervo, Sardinia, developed by the Aga Khan, has become a haven for yachts of every description.

Portofino, Italy has one of the most exquisite harbors in the world.

Cannes, in the south of France is renowned for the film festival, the jet set, and megayachts.

waiting for *Nabila*, we went to the Veteran Boat Rally in Porto Cervo. Walking down the dock at the end of a race, we saw many familiar yachts. *Escapade*, which had been in our first book, had just won a race and the owners asked us to come have some wine and celebrate, and as I sat in the comfortable main salon, I felt as if I could have be in Newport, R.I., or perhaps in St. Barts. Such is the beauty of yachting.

Another yacht recommended to us by Mark and Mike from Castlemain Yacht Brokers in Antibes was *Rio Rita*. We endeavored to meet John Warren at Feadship and thus gain entry to *Rio Rita*. As we awaited permission we learned that another yacht on our list, *Vagabunda*, was in our vicinity. We chased *Vagabunda* from port to port until we finally caught up with her in St. Tropez where we arrived just before sunset, confident of photographing her the next morning. But when we called to confirm the time of our appointment, we found that the yacht was leaving at dawn. So we pulled ourselves together to shoot her that evening.

In other corners of the world we had been tracking down the motor yacht *Jezebel*, whom we first encountered in Brooklyn, owned by Robert Stigwood. After a plethora of telephone calls we found out that the boat would be in Cherbourg the next day. The morning of our appointment, however, we were still in Monte Carlo speaking with the captain of *P'tit Louis* and *Bugs*, who assured us that the owner would change his mind about appearing in our book if we photographed both yachts and sent prints to the owner. Also, Tony Morgan, a yacht photographer, wanted us to view some of his work that same morning. Somehow we did it all, dashed to the Nice airport just in time, and after rent-a-cars, planes, taxis, and trains, we arrived in Cherbourg at past midnight where we assumed the captain or someone from *Jezebel* would meet us. There was no sign of anyone, not even a taxi. I queried a nice-looking man and his wife who had been on the train from Paris and who were also waiting for a taxi. In my barely adequate French I learned that the gentleman was the agent for *Jezebel*. What luck! Still, all of the hotels in Cherbourg were "complet." We waited in the lobby of one likely prospect until 1:15 a.m. Finally, a cognac or two later,

the concierge was certain his last reservation would not show. We got the last room. We slept, awoke, called *Jezebel* bright and early, and were told that they had to go on sea trial and could not give us clearance to go while they tested their new engines. Apologetic, and friendly, the crew did allow us a viewing of the yacht. Dana brought her camera gear along, just in case, but was told to leave it in the car, as we would only have a short time before they were due to depart. A member of the crew borrowed the car and took with him all of the camera equipment. Hours later, we were still on board, cameraless, and there would have been time after all. Tomorrow was out of the question, for the owner was arriving with guests.

Our last day before returning for the States, we decided to try *Nabila* again, just for the hell of it. Sure enough, we were told we should fly back to Nice the next day. Where will the boat be? Oh, Monaco, Antibes, or Cannes. We called again from the familiar Nice airport. The boat was in Monaco, and we had an appointment at 5:00 p.m. We drove the lovely coast road past Villefranche, and arrived at the dock at ten minutes to five. We brushed our hair, freshened our lipstick, and made it to the gang plank at five minutes to five. The deckhands were casting off the dock lines— the boat was her way to Antibes. Back in the car, back down the road, we felt like the Keystone Cops. But we did enjoy the view of Villefranche from the coast road and after all, we hadn't been to Antibes in weeks...

All in all, it has been an adventure, and we found the crew, various designers, builders, stylists, brokers, and owners all interesting and enthusiastic. The contributions by several designers reflect the individualism in yacht design today, and the different perspectives and ideas behind yachting. The yachts in this book cover a spectrum of tastes, but they all have one thing in common—they are all extraordinary.

Jill Bobrow

Jill Bobrow
President
Concepts Publishing

Introduction

Jill Bobrow and Dana Jinkins first came into my life—indirectly, I must add—when one St. Georges Day, which is also my birthday, about six copies of their previous book, *Classic Yacht Interiors* arrived as gifts from a diverse group of sailing purists. I kept one, and those that did not have rude remarks on the fly, suggesting which direction my boat building efforts should take, made excellent gifts for other enthusiasts.

Due to the fact that I am a professional of the yachting industry and over the last twenty-five years or so have had access to a fascinating variety of different types of yachts, I have come to appreciate and enjoy a wide range of craft from twelve-foot national dinghies to 250-foot motor yachts.

An enthusiast of yachts I am, and so obviously are Jill and Dana. Although the *Classic Yacht Interiors* book, now affectionately known as that green book, perhaps portrays these women as old sail boat fanatics, this new book of theirs is a much more difficult subject to approach. There are a wide variety of yacht types and real life design personalities, requiring interviews with many of the architects, stylists and decorators which make up the world of modern large yachting.

In producing a largely pictorial book Jill and Dana have avoided the technical controversy which often surrounds these so-called "megayachts" and have produced another thoroughly readable compendium of yachts which I am sure will keep the enthusiast enthused and convert some would-be owners to actual ownership.

George Nicholson

George Nicholson
Yacht Developer/Yacht Broker/Consultant
Mega Yacht Afficionado

Acajou

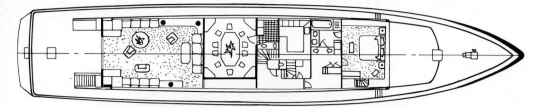

Acajou, owned by a Saudi Arabian, has the largest varnished hull in the world. Launched in 1983 by Les Chantiers Navals De L'Esterel, she was designed in collaboration with naval architect André Mauric. Flexible and resistant, the hull is triple-planked close-grained mahogany, glued without caulking. A thick external coat of extra strong resin protects it from worms and borers. Berthed in Cannes among a flotilla of basic run-of-the-mill "white" megayachts, *Acajou* truly stands out as unique.

The interior accommodation was designed by Jon Bannenberg. The modular forms and high-tech ambience create an ultramodern main salon. The colors are crisp creams and whites. The aft salon is dominated by a U-shaped white leather couch and a padded overhead. The configuration of the salon is totally conducive to entertainment, including a game table, video/stereo unit, and a well stocked movie library. The dining salon is amidships, and includes an oval table that seats ten on cane, wood, and stainless steel tubular chairs with comfortable leather cushions.

The large owners' cabin is situated forward on the main deck. A padded headboard behind the double bed rises to a padded ceiling. Another entertainment unit faces the bed. And for further fun and games, there is a two-and-a-half meter square Jacuzzi bath. The cabin has burgundy accents to the ubiquitous white tones. Using only one color per room (one of the guest rooms uses gold as the accent color) preserves the overall clean, modern design.

There is an observation salon, and an enormous sun deck with shower, bar, heated towel cupboard and an outside dining table in front of the docking platform and mast. Besides being a beautiful yacht, *Acajou* features a couple of turbo-charged MTU 16 cylinder diesels that enable her to top out at just over 35 knots— quite fast for a 42-meter yacht!

MIKE MEADE

MIKE MEADE

MIKE MEADE

Type: Motor Yacht
LOA: 137′6″/42m
Beam: 25′5″/7.75m
Draft: 6′7″/2.1m
Displacement: 165 metric tons
Designer: Jon Bannenberg/Interior
Builder: Chantiers de l'Esterel
Year: 1983
Hull: Mahogany
Engine: MTU 16V 538 TB 92/
7340HP
Cruising speed: 15-30 knots
Max Speed: 35 knots

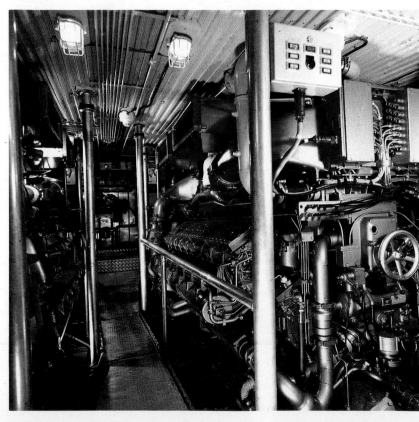

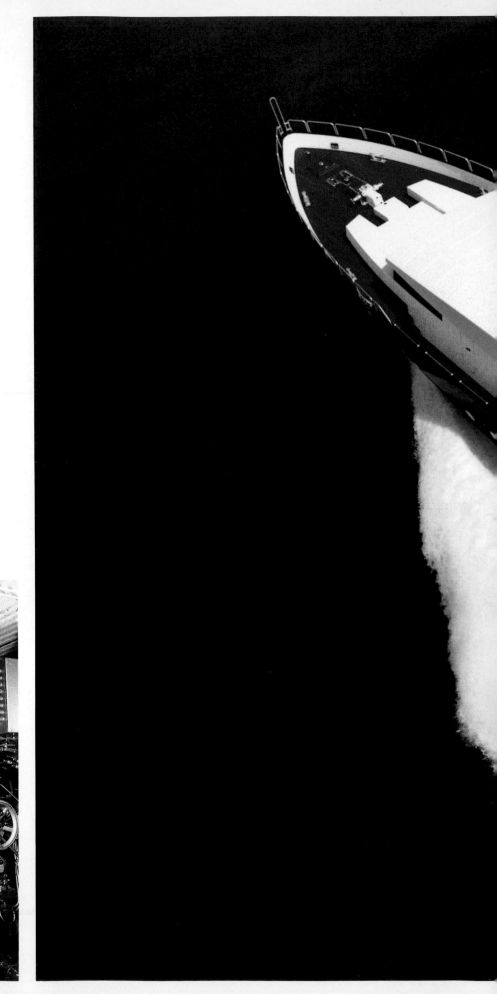

Acajou

Al Kumait

Al Kumait, a high speed motor cruiser was named after a famous race horse. With all of the styling done by Terry Disdale, she became the prototype for the Tarquin Gulf 50. This particular yacht was designed for Usamah Ziad Al Kazemi, a businessman from Kuwait who had a very specific idea of what he wanted. The 50-foot cruiser is fully air-conditioned and has an enormous salon that extends the full width of the boat through a design innovation. The side decks were eliminated in favor of staircases running over the boat.

The interior is fitted with specially designed wool carpet woven in Ireland, leather and suede furnishings and highly polished Lebanese burr walnut. Al Kazemi disdains the sight of nuts, bolts and hinges so these are all cunningly concealed; the doors open as if by magic. Every detail on the boat was custom designed.

Other special features include a freezer set in the cockpit, an hydraulically operated table that disappears into the floor, an auto pilot and remote control system which almost eliminates the need for crew. The galley unit is unique in that it can be pulled out into the aft cockpit and when not in use can totally disappear from sight. Most striking is the luxurious master stateroom with its seven-foot circular bed complete with fur bedspread. After all, the cruiser was designed strictly for having fun!

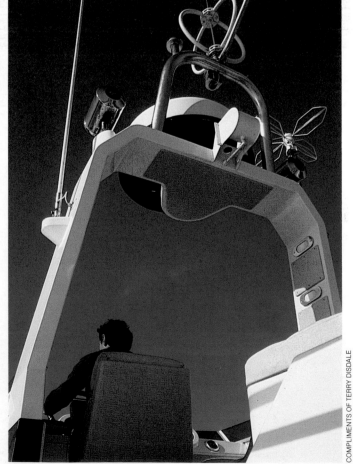

COMPLIMENTS OF TERRY DISDALE

Type: Motor Cruiser
LOA: 52'10"/16.1m
Beam: 15'2"/4.6m
Draft: 3'3"/1.0m
Displacement: 14 tons
Designer/Stylist: Terry Disdale
Hull designer: Bernard Olesinski
Builder: Tarquin Boat Company, England
Hull: Fiberglass
Engines: Twin turbocharged Volvo Penta TAMD 70D

COMPLIMENTS OF TERRY DISDALE

Alma

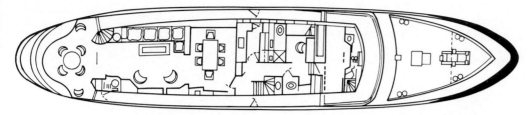

Type: Motor Yacht
LOA: 108'/33m
Beam: 22'/6.7m
Draft: 7'/2.2m
Designer: H.W. de Voogt &
    Zn., Haarlem
Builder: C. vanLent & Zonen Kaag,
    Holland
Year: 1970
Hull: Steel
Engine: 2 Cat D343's, 460HP

lma is a lovely Feadship. She was originally built as a transition from a sailboat to a motor yacht. The year she was launched, 1970, was the year of a TransPac race, and the owner used her as a kind of committee boat to follow the race to Hawaii. Therefore, *Alma* was built to cross the Pacific, and is very self-sufficient, with large fuel storage, watermaking capabilities, and 7,000-mile cruising range.

The aft deck is protected from the sun and separated from the main salon by wood trimmed glass doors. The round glass table is surrounded by large rattan and cane chairs. The custom wool carpet, evident throughout the boat, is particularly eye-catching on the aft deck. The underwater motif of crustaceans and coral is presented in a variety of browns, greens, and sand colors.

The main salon is similarly appointed in subdued earth tones with an L-shaped couch upholstered in a rich dark brown bull leather. A slight Oriental flavor is given by the coffee table, throw pillows, the three lacquered panels behind the dining room table, and the various paintings in the passageways. Both the dining area and the main salon are flanked by sizeable picture windows which create an airy feeling. To further enhance that sense of lightness and openness, the teak wall panelling has been limed and coated with a satin varnish. The general effect is clean and contemporary without being cold or in any way antiseptic.

Guest staterooms for six and the crew's quarters are on the lower deck level. Two of the staterooms have twin beds and the master stateroom has a king-size bed. They all have private bathrooms with gold-plated sinks and faucets. Floor to ceiling mirrors enhance the space in the staterooms. The master stateroom echoes the underwater theme of the carpet on the aft deck. The back drop behind the bed's headboard is a scene of shells and coral, also reflected in the bedspread and curtains. Recessed lighting from the ceiling focuses on the art work.

The boat deck carries two launches as expected on a yacht of this size and caliber. What is not expected is the automobile, transferred from deck to shore by davits. It is one of the six Shellettes converted from a Fiat 850, replete with wicker seats. The owners have enjoyed the car from Cutty Hunk to Peter Island.

Al Riyadh

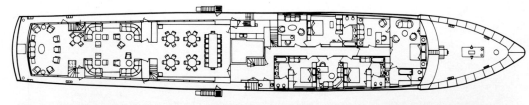

Type: Motor Yacht
LOA: 212′1″/64.64m
LWL: 195′11″/59.72m
Beam: 31′10″/9.7m
Draft: 10′3″/3.13m
Designer: F. de Voogt
Interior Designer: Pierre Tanter
Builder: Feadship
Year: 1978
Hull: Steel
Engine: 2 MTU Diesel, Model 16V956
TB71 / 3150 hp each at 1500 rpm
Speed: 20 knots

NATIONAL PHOTO PERSBUREAU

*A*l *Riyadh,* as the name suggests, has a distinctly Arabian flavor, particularly in the upper deck lounge which is designed to resemble an Arabian tent. Frits de Voogt designed the yacht for the late King Khalid of Saudi Arabia. The yacht was built at the Van Lent Yard and took nearly two and a half years to complete. This floating palace is equipped with everything from a hair dressing salon to a fully equipped intensive care unit, including complete X-ray equipment. Khalid, who suffered from a heart ailment, wanted to insure that he was never far from emergency care.

Pierre Tanter, who designed the interior, used light oak with bronze and stainless steel ornaments. The king often catered to a vast number of people, so space was of paramount importance in the reception rooms and lounges. The dining room accommodates forty people. The tentlike upper deck lounge has blue and white striped material overhead as well as on the bulkheads and the furniture.

NATIONAL PHOTO PERSBUREAU

Aquarius

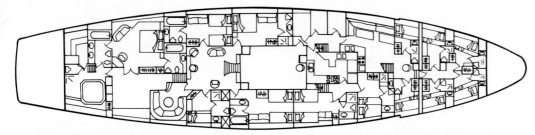

Type: Three-masted schooner
LOA: 175'/53.3m
LOD: 156'/47.5m
Beam: 32'/9.8m
Draft: 12'5"/3.8m
Designer: Henry J. Gielow; redesigned by James M. Stoll
Builder: Bath Iron Works, Bath, Maine; rebuilt: Abeking & Rasmussen, Lemwerder, W. Germany
Year: 1930; **rebuilt:** 1983
Hull: Steel
Engine: 2 Volvo Pentas TAMD 120B/360 HP at 1800 RPM
Sail area: 11,400 sq ft.

FRED DOVASTON

*A*quarius was launched in 1930 for the Roeblings, who were most noted for the construction of the Brooklyn Bridge. She was built to Lloyds 100 A1 standards at Bath Iron Works in Bath, Maine along with other fine yachts of that era, and christened *Black Douglas*, after a Scottish Highlander of legend, meaning "dark water" in Gaelic.

Mr. Roebling kept the yacht eleven years, much of the time at his private island after an adventurous trip around Cape Horn. In 1941 *Black Douglas* was purchased by Congressional appropriation. She was sent on a seal protection mission to Alaska but the trip was cut short after she was fired upon by an enemy submarine off the California coast just ten days after the bombing of Pearl Harbor.

She became a patrol vessel of the United States Navy when the U.S. entered the war and she suffered the embarrassment of having her rig removed. After the war, she was turned over to the fish and wildlife service and began a new life, first tracking fur seals in Alaska and later participating in fishery research which lasted for ten years.

In the early 1960s, she was sold at auction to a treasure hunter who depleted his pocket book without nourishment from Davy Jones' locker. The result was that after seven years of riding at anchor, the *Black Douglas* was purchased in 1972 for use as a school ship and renamed *Te Quest*. Two major overhauls were completed to return her sailing rig according to the original plans and to fit her out with classrooms.

For the next nine years she sailed alongside the yacht *Te Vega* voyaging throughout the Caribbean, Mediterranean, North and Baltic Seas, along the coast of Africa and far up the Amazon, under the flag of the Flint School.

In 1982 she was sold again and, under a private owner's flag, she was taken to Abeking & Rasmussen where she was completely gutted, her plating renewed, and totally rebuilt from the frames up. She was then redesigned by James M. Stoll, a former owner, who conceived, organized, and supervised the construction of a unique multi-level interior comprising seven double guest cabins with baths, an owners' suite with six person spa and sauna, an office, living and bedroom with his and hers bath. There is also a library, enclosed sunken wheelhouse, two bars, two galleys and six double crew cabins with baths.

In the machine room he placed twin engines, watermakers, full air conditioning and three generators to service the ship. *Aquarius* has twenty-two phone connections linked to satellite, telefax, telex, and the most sophisticated navigational aids in the wheelhouse. Interior and deckhouse styling was done by Abeking & Rasmussen according to concept artwork by John Munford, and interior appointments were arranged by Els Stoll. The yacht is currently class A-1 with the American Bureau of Shipping.

Thus, after a rich and varied life, *Aquarius* is once again used exclusively as a private yacht. But one problem still exists: *Aquarius's* masts, at 131 feet, are too tall to fit the Brooklyn Bridge, which reaches 127 feet!

Aquarius

Australia II

Type: Twelve Meter Sloop
LOA: 64'/19.51m
LWL: 44'/13.41m
Beam: 12'3"/3.73m
Draft: 8'8"/2.53m
Builder: S.E. Ward & Co.
Cottesloe, Perth, Australia
Designer: Ben Lexcen

ustralia II revolutionized the America's Cup Competition and in fact nearly created a revolution. She is the reason that after 132 years of winning, the legendary America's Cup has been handed over to the Royal Perth Yacht Club. *Australia II* is a Ben Lexcen design that has been considered highly unusual. It is a light displacement *Twelve* (about 51,500 lbs.) that has a cutaway underbody with almost no skeg and a strangely shaped "upside down" keel. It is broader at the base than at the top and has wings about six feet long and three feet wide angled down about twenty feet from it. This winged keel created a great deal of controversy during the trials, in 1983, when the New York Yacht Club challenged the keel design. Since her draft increased as she heeled, the Yacht Club argued that she might have rated more than 12 meters. The Club lost the protest.

Lexcen wanted to produce a *Twelve* that would be quick to turn off the starting line. He designed *Australia II* with the minimum allowed waterline length of 44 feet and the minimum displacement. Therefore, she tacks like a dinghy in a tight arc and has less resistance to turning than the other *Twelves*. It is the wings on the keel that provided the necessary resistance to slipping sideways. Her turning, acceleration and pointing were all exceptional. The keel shape was kept secret and hidden from onlookers throughout the race. When hauled, plastic curtained her charms. Ben Lexcen is seen clowning here, perhaps he is demonstrating how his keel design can be used as a surf board.

The history-making year was Alan Bond's fourth America's Cup challenge. He had a strong team: John Bertrand a Finn Olympic medalist, Soling champion and experienced ocean racer, at the helm, Sir James Hardy, skipper of three previous Australian challengers as backup helmsman, and Hugh Treharne, a sailmaker, as tactician.

Liberty and *Australia II* were quite evenly matched to windward. Liberty tended to gain slightly on the reaches, but usually lost to *Australia II* while tacking and running. The America's Cup competition had the distinction of successfully staving off twenty-four challenges. This was probably an unprecedented occurrence in the history of sports. The first defense of the Cup was in 1870 when James Ashbury's 108-foot schooner, *Cambria*, was the sole foreign challenger racing a fleet of American sloops and schooners around a Sandy Hook, New York course. She lost to Franklin Osgood's schooner *Magic* by a margin of 39 minutes, 12 seconds.

On September 24, 1983, *Australia II* finished the 7th and final race of the America's Cup just 41 seconds ahead of *Liberty*. The top left photograph shows *Liberty* and *Australia II* neck and neck.

BARRY STEVENS

DAN NERNEY

TED KELLEY, PHOTO-BOAT

Azteca

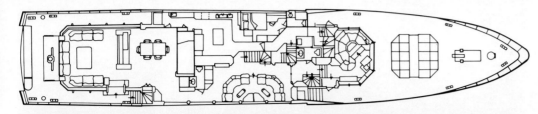

Type: Motor Yacht
LOA: 147'/44.8m
LWL: 120'4"/36.7
Beam: 27'7"/8.4m
Draft: 8'2"/2.5m
Designer: Jon Bannenberg, Ltd., London
Naval Architects: H. W. de Voogt & Son, Haarlem, Holland
Builder: Feadship, Holland
Hull: Steel
Engines: 2 M.T.U. Marine Diesels, Mode 16V538, TB82, 2950 hp each at 1760 rpm
Speed: 22 knots

NATIONAL FOTO PERSBUREAU

NATIONAL PHOTO PERSBUREAU

Azteca was built as one of a pair of new yachts for a Central American based international businessman. *Azteca* is both fast and truly revolutionary. The hull was designed by de Voogt at Feadship and the exterior styling and the interior design were done by Jon Bannenberg. The yacht was built at de Vries, one of the two Feadship yards in Holland. Her totally unique look is attributed to her "high sides," and what has been called "the greenhouse effect." The main hull goes clear up to the top deck, breaking with the traditional yacht look. Although many people are shocked by such a radical approach, this design is not mere spurious affectation, but rather is intended to utilize the full beam of the yacht to maximum advantage. Bannenberg defends his unusual design by pointing out how well it works. He says he has been on board when fifty or sixty people disappear due to the many comfortable and different lounges on the boat.

The top deck features an enclosed glass-roofed and air conditioned solarium as well as an owners' suite on two decks culminating in a private observation area on the main deck forward. The interior makes use of pale birds-eye maple veneer combined with padded overheads of kid leather. Many of the bulkheads are covered in fabrics of silk and cotton specially woven for the yacht. Thick wool carpets of the finest sock yarn, also handmade, cover the cabin soles. The quilted effect adds a measure of extreme comfort.

Besides the luxurious owner stateroom/lounge, there are three double guest staterooms, each with private bathrooms. There are two salons, one amidships and one aft. There is a formal dining room forward of the aft salon, and an upper deck lounge and bar.

The crew's quarters are totally separate and private from the rest of the boat, insuring maximum privacy for the owner and his guests.

If this yacht doesn't simply take your breath away, perhaps you'll be impressed by seeing *Azteca* alongside *Paraiso*, her sistership which belongs to the same owner. When the two cruise in tandem, the double whammy effect is truly awesome.

JON BANNENBERG

NATIONAL PHOTO PERSBUREAU

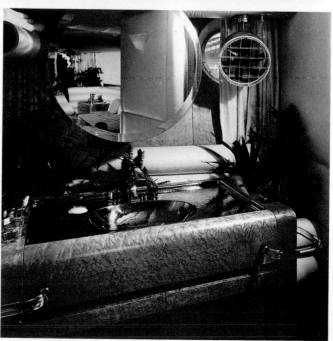

NATIONAL FOTO PERSBUREAU

Blue Horizon IV

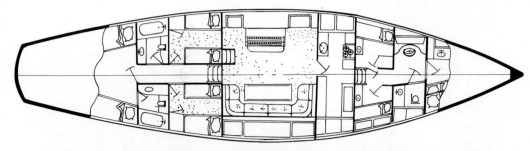

COMPLIMENTS OF MR. R. CHALK

Type: Ketch rigged twin screw
  motor sailer
LOA: 99'/30.18m
LWL: 66'/20.2m
Beam: 21'4"/6.5m
Draft: 12'4"/3.8m
Tonnage: 114.20 gross/ 71.13 net/
  TM 134
Builder/Designer: Camper &
  Nicholsons, Ltd.
Year: 1960/rebuilt 1979-80
Hull: Steel
Engine: 2 Mercedes Benz V-10
  Diesels OM403/450bhp each, Twin
  Disc reverse reduction gears, type
  MG509, ratio 2:1
Cruising speed: 11 knots

*B*lue Horizon IV, built by Camper & Nicholson in 1960, is a most unusually appointed motorsailer. Noticeable at first glance is the spacious and protected on-deck lounge and dining area separated from the wheelhouse by a plexiglass partition. This space, with very large opening windows, was customized by the owners in 1979.

Below decks was constructed and decorated in 1979-80. Descending the companionway, one does not have the sensation of being on a sailboat. No built-in cupboards and teak panelling here. Although the dining table is gimballed, there is no other nautical reminder in the furnishings. The owners, an American businessman and his wife, travel extensively around the world and have accumulated various artifacts, particularly from Korea, Thailand, China, and India, evidence of which is omnipresent. Cupboards have been fabricated from Oriental screens, tapestries cover the bulkheads, and antique masks add to the exotica. The main salon also features a Yamaha organ which does not even require a player in order to produce a full orchestra.

The galley and crew's quarters are forward of the main salon and have private access. The galley was also rebuilt in 1979, accommodating a large walk-in deep freeze and a washer/dryer and more storage shelves.

Aft of the main salon, descending six steps off a central passageway is a double guest stateroom to port. The room is decorated with a wildly patterned bedspread and matching fabric wallpaper. A black lacquered dresser adds to the dramatics of the room. Opposite is a single guest stateroom with a blue flowered motif that is repeated throughout, including the overhead ceiling. The guest bathroom enjoys a full length bathtub, and Sherle Wagner washbasin with gold fixtures.

The after passageway terminates at the master stateroom which extends the full width of the boat. There are four opening ports and a large overhead skylight. Again the decor is replete with collectibles from around the world. The master head is tiled and also has a bathtub and gold-plated washbasin and fixtures.

Blue Horizon is strictly a family boat, and has been refined to suit the very particular taste of the owners. She spends a lot of time in Monaco.

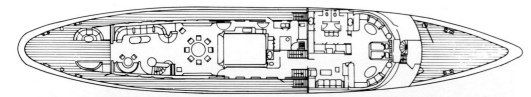

Type: Motor Yacht
LOA: 166'/50.6m
Beam: 27'/8.2m
Designer: G. De Jorio
Built: Italy/rebuilt: Luerssen Co.,
Bremen, W. Germany
Year: 1964/rebuilt: 1985
Hull: Steel
Main Engines: 2 X MTU 1350 hp
each
Cruise speed: 15 knots
Cruise range: up to 5700 sm

*B*lue Shadow is available for charter in the Caribbean in the winter and in the Mediterranean in the summer. She can accommodate up to twelve guests, all in double staterooms with private baths. The competent, multilingual crew of thirteen run the yacht in true Bristol fashion. Formerly named *New Horizon C, Blue Shadow,* built in 1964, underwent an extensive refit and reconstruction in 1985. The original bridgedeck was cut off, and the bridge housing and the bow were both extended. The conversion was done in Bremen, West Germany, and resulted in a truly efficient, immaculate yacht representing the highest standards of German craftmanship and engineering.

The South Pacific seems to be a theme throughout the main salon and staterooms. Everything is beige and turquoise, reflecting a tropical sea. The feeling of light and sunshine is accented by the creamy ultrasuede overhead, inlaid with a mirrored panel and recessed lighting. The large dining table is fabricated with an unusual plasticized parchment and surrounded by pillow-stuffed armchairs. The spacious living room is also equipped with an organ for the musically inclined.

The master stateroom is on the main deck level forward of the main salon. It is preceded by a cozy yet roomy study. The spacious master bedroom even has an unusual walk-in closet hidden behind curtains. The guest staterooms all have appealing names of romantic islands such as "Fiji" and "Maui."

The on deck galley is quite spacious with a special gadget for Chinese cooking, one of the owners' favorite culinary tastes. The whole yacht is thoroughly modern.

The boat deck is expansive and terrific for large parties. The sundeck features bright yellow cushions and yellow lounge chairs, all in keeping with the themes of sun and sea.

M.P. ANDREW

Blue Shadow

Britannia

Type: Ship
LOA: 412′3″/125m
LBP: 360′/109m
LWL: 380′/115m
Beam: 54′6″/16m
Depth: 32′6″/10m
Load Displacement: 4,715 tons
Gross tonnage: 5,769 tons
Engines: Twin geared steam turbines as developed by John Brown and Parsons Marine Eng. Res. and Dev. Assoc./12000 shaft HP producing a continuous speed of 21 knots @ 286 rpm
Builder: John Brown & Co. (Clydebank) Ltd.
Year: 1954

ritannia was designed by Sir Victor Shepheard, K.C.B., the director of Naval Construction, with the dual role of Royal Yacht during peacetime and, in the event of war, a hospital ship. The order was officially placed with John Brown in February 1952 and the keel was laid in June of that year. Her Majesty Queen Elizabeth launched the vessel on April 16, 1953 and the *Britannia* was completed and accepted by the Admiralty on January 11, 1954.

The *Britannia,* from her gold-banded blue hull to her interior, is a very proper yacht. Princess Anne and Mark Phillips, and Charles and Diana spent their respective honeymoons onboard. Sometimes she has more serious business, such as rescuing refugees from South Yemen. She is pictured here dockside at the mountainous island of St. Vincent in the Grenadines, West Indies.

Contrary to popular belief, the yacht belongs not to the Queen, but to the Ministry of Defence. Her captain is a Rear Admiral. She has traveled over 700,000 miles to visit the Commonwealth over the years. She is maintained by 277 crew when the Queen is onboard, and they all wear uniforms designed by Queen Victoria.

The interior is comfortable with an eclectic array of decor. The anteroom which leads into the drawing-room is bright and light featuring overstuffed couches and chairs. There is a piano off to one side but the focal point of this room is the oil painting above the mantel. The sitting room has a comfortable looking pale green velvet sofa and a long, no-nonsense working desk. Over the faux fireplace is a circular gilded antique mirror. The sunroom, with floor-to-ceiling windows at one end, has narrow panelled walls and two blue flowered settees. The dining room has several long tables arranged in a conversational grouping, and is perhaps reminiscent of a favorite dining establishment outside of London somewhere. It is both traditional and formal, yet unprepossessing. In fact, the whole of the interior of *Britannia* is the quintessence of British heritage—nothing nouveau or flashy here—and of a quiet elegance and a refined sense of functional comfort.

Buckpasser

Buckpasser is the first of a series of motor yachts built by Hitachi Zosen, Japan. Hitachi Zosen has over one hundred years of experience in ship building and other industrial fields, but this project has opened up a new world for them and for the owner of the *Buckpasser*. The yard at Kanagawa is all business, the same sophistication employed in building supertankers is utilized in the construction of a mere 120-footer. The laying of the keel in any large yacht usually is a ceremonious occasion. In Japan, it is a time for the Buddhist priest to come and bless the yacht.

The skipper of *Buckpasser* has worked for the owner of the boat for twelve years. Therefore, it was natural that he be present at much of the construction. The yacht, quiet and comfortable, is equipped with the most advanced electronics and computer systems. She was built strictly for family cruising. Launched in the fall of 1985, she was then shipped to the United States where her interior was fine tuned.

The main salon is painted a brilliant evergreen, with mahogany trim and white overheads. The sofas and settees are upholstered in a bright floral pattern. All of the colors are extremely bold. Prominent in the salon is the elephant, but there are quite a few other collectibles around the peripheries. The dining salon features a well conceived wine cellar.

Accommodations include two master staterooms and two guest cabins. All of the staterooms are painted and decorated with matching bedspreads and wallpaper. The gameroom on the main deck offers an opportunity for the grandchildren to enjoy themselves away from the adults, and vice versa.

The skipper who has taken the yacht cruising through the Caribbean says all systems work well and that the family is planning a trip to the Pacific.

COMPLIMENTS OF HITACHI ZOSEN

Type: Motor Yacht
LOA: 121′4″/36.99m
Beam: 25′4″/7.72m
Draft: 6′6″/1.97m
Designer: Jack B. Hargrave
Builder: Hitachi Zosen Corporation,
    Japan (Kanagawa Works)
Year: 1985
Hull: Aluminum
Engines: Twin Caterpillar 3508TA
    Turbocharged Diesels/600hp each

Bugs

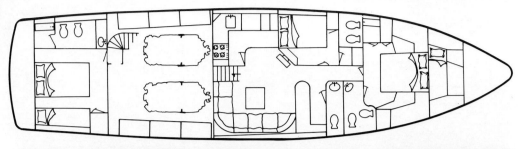

Type: High Speed Motor Yacht
LOA: 65'6''/20m
LWL: 64'4''/19.6m
Beam: 17'/5.20m
Draft: 5'6''/1.7m
Displacement: 42 tons
Designer: Aldo Chichero
Builder: Mondomarine, Cunco, Italy
Year: 1984
Hull: Fiberglass /Kevlar
Engines: Isota Fraschini/1520 hp
Gross tons: 66.37; net tons: 30.23

*B*ugs is a very fast motor yacht built by Mondomarine in Italy. She is a super deluxe high-tech pleasure craft, used primarily to get somewhere fast.

Bugs is one of a series of Aldo Chichero's "America" designs. She is twenty meters, forty metric tons fully loaded, and capable of forty knots. The design is a variation on the idea of an open cruiser with true flexibility in terms of closing and shielding the deck space. Protection is provided by a simple modular coachroof. The open deck level is screened only by a windshield, side windows, and the roll bar. Soft moveable closure panels are connected to this area and a glass partition behind the helm. The aft sundeck is an expansive uninterrupted space.

She is all silver on deck, even the sunning cushions are silver. The transom gate is cleverly designed to open on one end, and swivel out to act as the gang plank.

The accommodations are slick and modern, silver gray is the main motif with magenta as an accent color. Everything is built in and designed to withstand high-speed cruising. When you are flying off to Sardinia at 35 to 40 knots, the T.V. will be secure in a flexible shock resistant encasement. Also the crystal flower vase is affixed permanently and will not topple over. Color coordination is omnipresent. The Gaggia espresso maker is even painted silver. The ceiling has a flock of hand-painted seagulls reminiscent of a Max Escher motif.

The master stateroom also has a hand-painted ceiling and leather zigzag sculptured panelling on the walls. The bulkheads are water tight compartments and there is an escape hatch in the master stateroom. The galley is compact and fully equipped with everything you would need for an extended trip.

Bugs is equipped with extremely sophisticated instrumentation. The Furuno FCR 1411 color-readout radar has an anti-collision alarm. There is also a Loran Furuno LC 80, a Furuno FE606 echo-sounder with digital graphic readout, an autopilot with ETC aeronautical compass, and a two speed Seiem Hytron helm. Furthermore, this impressive array of "navionics" is almost completely doubled; the identical twin instrument is a safety feature.

Bugs belongs to the same owner as the yacht *P'tit Louis* (also featured in this book) and is managed by Navigator of Monte Carlo.

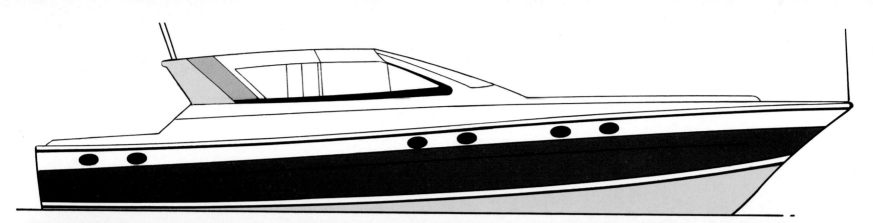

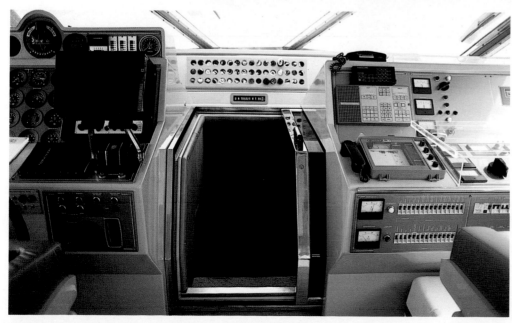

Calliope

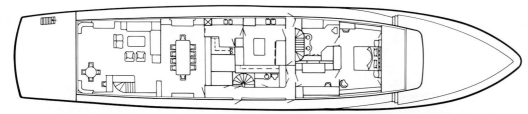

Type: Motor Yacht
LOA: 145'/44m
Beam: 29'/8.83m
Draft: 8'6"/2.59m
Displacement: 325 metric tons
Hull: Aluminum
Engines: 2 X Caterpillar 3512 TA, 1300 hp each
Builder: Hitachi Zosen, Japan
Designer: Hargrave
Interior Designer: Pierre Tanter
Year: 1986

ROY MONTGOMERY

ROY MONTGOMERY

Calliope, belonging to Edgar Kaiser, Jr. is a 148-foot Hargrave-designed aluminum boat built at the Hitachi Zosen Yard in Japan. Edgar Kaiser, Jr. built his first boat from a plywood kit and sailed it to Alaska when he was twelve years old.

Mr. Kaiser's grandfather, the famed industrialist Mr. Henry J. Kaiser, was best known in boating circles for the Liberty ships which he turned out by the hundreds during World War II. He and his son built boats which ranged from 200 mile per hour unlimited hydroplanes to over one hundred-foot sailing catamarans. At the same time, they began the family tradition, now in its third generation, of building a veritable fleet of family cruising boats. In each of these boats, the Kaisers have always incorporated the successful features of previous boats, redesigned things which did not work well, and at the same time moved forward with new and innovative design features.

Edgar Kaiser, Jr. is a do-it-yourself yachtsman. He and his family have cruised, without crew, the West Coast and Alaska extensively in their former 78-foot Hargrave designed yacht, which was also named *Calliope*. With the new *Calliope*, the Kaiser's cruising grounds are now worldwide; their maiden voyage was from Tokyo to Honolulu.

With satellite telephone and telex, Mr. Kaiser's business activities can be handled from anywhere in the world. Furthermore, Mr. Kaiser's private jet, which he pilots himself, makes intermittent travel to the yacht a snap.

The interior of *Calliope* was designed by Pierre Tanter to be modern, clean and efficient. The main salon is panelled in a Japanese wood; sen. The unusual coffee table, designed especially for *Calliope* by Tanter has a

bone rim and exhibits, beneath glass, a map of the two hemispheres and crossed flags bearing the burgee of the Royal Vancouver Yacht Club and the signal flag for the letter "K."

The accommodations include an owners' stateroom forward on the main deck with whirlpool bath, a large walk-in closet and a separate den. Four double staterooms with large complete baths accommodate eight guests. For entertainment there is an integrated television system with 19 television receivers and 3 video cassette recorder/players and just as many stereo units.

The boat deck has a hot tub and a lounge area. Curvaceous, built-in seats face a rather extraordinary coffee table constructed around an antique merry-go-round horse, which has become a kind of trademark aboard several of the Kaisers' yachts.

Modern efficiency is another Kaiser trademark, and *Calliope* is a beautiful realization of the family's ideals.

Designer's Notes

I was born in Brittany in the western part of France, a place we Bretons call "the end of the world." Most people there live from the sea. My father was a sailor, my grandfather was a sailor, and I've always had a great interest in boats– all kinds of boats.

I started my career as a designer after World War II in Cannes. Early on I concentrated on houses and apartments on the Côte d'Azur. Since Cannes is obviously a very attractive place for yachting, I had the opportunity to meet yacht owners, and I became involved in designing yacht interiors.

Of paramount importance is to establish a good rapport with the yacht owners. Most of my clients are extraordinary people and it is always fascinating to me to listen to their ideas and find a way to implement what they would like. When I design a yacht, I keep in mind the four most important aspects. First of all, proportion. The size and height of rooms on boats are quite different from houses and require a great deal of attention. Secondly, colors. I never use "heavy" colors, except as accents. Here again, the taste of the owners is very important, and I don't try to impose a color upon them if they do not like it. Third is lighting. It must be very well-balanced. Last are the details, the focal points, etc. I take very great interest in small details, such as special bronze cast ornaments, or an owner's personal effects. Overall, comfort is, of course, of tremendous importance and must be produced without spoiling proportions.

Perhaps the most fulfilling aspect of my work is the "spirit" of the team, including the naval architect, the yard, and the working people. All of us are always proud of our yacht. We are filled with emotion when the yacht is finally launched because it has been a part of our lives for so many months.

Pierre Tanter

When I think of yachting, I think of the romance of the sea that has long lured and fascinated man. When I begin designing, I approach the project with this thought in mind. This is the realm of personal desire.

My view of design as a total thought process comes from my background in the fine arts and in architecture. Each project brings a new set of requirements, and each outcome is different. Space planning is a three-dimensional concept balancing function, of traffic patterns and illusion, and the sheer aesthetics of luxury and beauty. Rotating these factors like a Rubic's Cube will bring balance and proportion to the shapes you want: an intriguing process that dictates direction.

Even the smallest details are calculated and must be done in the finest workmanship to make the whole concept a strong statement from the inside out. Like moving closer to a great painting, it gets better and better.

I begin by talking with clients to get a feeling of what the yacht is to them and what they want it to do for them. With this information as a basis, I can suggest ideas that extend and fully develop their initial concept. My mind is constantly manipulating multiple ideas and thoughts and rearranging them many times before I first put them on paper.

With this complete view of design I can take the clients from the first concept of hull and profile design into space planning and interior arrangements, down to furnishings and stationery and china design.

I do not consider designing my occupation. It is a continuous process. The process of creating is the challenge; the excitement is to see the idea come to life.

I try "never to say never." A client's request is an extension of their dream; after all, this is his fantasy.

Susan Puleo

FLIP AND DEBRA SCHULKE

Compass Rose

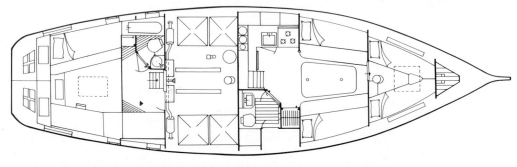

Compass Rose has become a famous fixture at Bowens Wharf in Newport, R.I. This colorful Nova Scotia Topsail schooner was originally a Brigantine rig. She was completed in 1970 although her vintage appearance is reminiscent of a pirate ship. Her character has led to several supporting film roles as well as a place in the Tall Ships Parade.

The owner, New Englander, Bob Entin, has a very close relationship with his yacht. He speaks about her as if she were human. He says she has a personality: she is warm, loving, romantic, and a movie star. The vessel was featured in a three dimensional movie made for St. Augustine's Marineland, and in a movie produced by a German film company. In the latter, the boat had to sail down Biscayne Bay with twelve children and no crew members showing. Entin admitted to being nervous about relying on his electronics system and no one but a German camera boat giving orders.

The boat was commissioned by Mimi Thygesen at the Nova Scotia Shipyard in 1969, where she took two years to build. She was sold to the late Herb Shriner, then purchased by Mr. Entin in 1975. He says, "It's a way of life, a work of art, a creation. I would really be upset if I ever had to sell her. I just can't think of being without her."

Mr. Entin likes compactness and the boat reflects a cozy intimacy. Panelled in a rich mahogany with leather-bound books in the bookshelves and high-lighted oil paintings and tapestry-like upholstery on the settees, the main cabin is dimly lit and cozy. The aft cabin enjoys the light from the transom windows that wrap around the stern of the boat and has a fold out table for navigation, and an impressive array of electronic equipment.

The *Compass Rose* travels every winter from Newport, R.I. to Florida. In the summer of 1986 she will join other Tall Ships to celebrate the anniversary of the Statue of Liberty.

Type: Topsail schooner
LOA: 60'/18.29m
LWL: 43'/13.10m
Beam: 14'/4.2m
Draft: 6'/1.82m
Year: 1969
Hull: Wood
Built: Nova Scotia

Delfino

Type: Motor Yacht
LOA: 103'/31.39m
Beam: 24'/7.31m
Draft: 10'/3.04m
Designer: Arthur DeFever
Interior Designer: Susan Puleo
Builder: Maritima De Axpe, Spain
Year: 1971
Hull: Steel
Engine: 2 U25 hp Caterpillar D-353
  diesels
Cruising speed: 10 knots
Max. speed: 12 knots

MICHAEL DeCOULOS

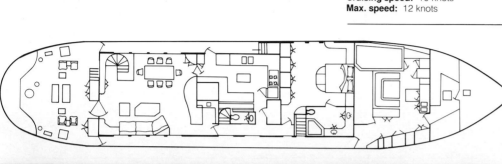

MICHAEL DeCOULOS

Delfino II was designed by Arthur DeFever to be a self-sufficient ocean-going motor yacht during voyages of up to six months and 12,000 miles. Built in 1971, she has recently undergone a two year major refit. All of the mechanics, including engines, generators, piping, and wiring, have been overhauled or replaced and the entire interior has been redecorated and refinished by Susan Puleo.

The main salon/dining area is Art Deco with basic colors of silver-gray accented in shades of fuchsia and lilac. The sculpted carpet is custom coordinated to match the color scheme. On entering the room through the starboard companionway there is a full wet serving bar, complete with oversized icemaker, sink, liquor racks, and flush cabinets. The counter and serving top is covered in blue granite. Recessed lighting illuminates the counter top and overhead is a mirrored lighted ceiling. The built-in furniture in the salon has been painted a metalic gray and Awlgripped. The glass and stainless steel dining table has dolphins carved into the base and is surrounded by custom leather chairs. Tucked into this high-tech Art Deco decor are a few eclectic surprises, such as an antique Chinese relief carving and a pair of two-hundred-year-old Thai temple pillars. Additional Chinese artifacts such as murals, carvings, screens, and scroll silk tapestries are used as accent pieces in the passageways and in the other staterooms.

There are five double staterooms; the four guest cabins are on the lower deck level. Two of the guest cabins can be converted to one large suite by removing the sound proof doors. The flow of colors and style are cohesive throughout the boat. The owners' stateroom is on the main deck forward of the main salon. The spacious suite is further enlarged by a mirrored bulkhead. Behind the mirrors are four closets, three of which are cedar-lined. The center closet contains a complete entertainment center. The king-size bed has an Art Deco designed headboard in custom-dyed fuchsia kid leather. At the foot of the bed are two silk ottomans with a hydraulically operated table between them. Behind the bed is iridescent wallpaper and a glass carving. The master bathroom has custom lilac and fuchsia tiles and a Carrera marble counter top. The vanity has been Awlgripped in silver while all of the fixtures are 24-karat gold. Not only are the dolphin fittings gold, but so are the toothbrush handles. Equally impressive is the bridge, which is decked out in a combination of black leather and chrome and with unique carved lucite throttle handles at the controls.

Delfino is completely outfitted for entertainment, comfort and pleasure, and includes three Boston Whalers, a Zodiac, and a Bell Jet Ranger III helicopter.

MICHAEL DeCOULOS

Dreamboat

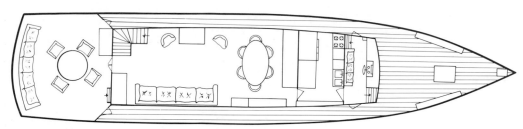

Type: Motor Yacht
LOA: 84'/25.60m
Beam: 19'/5.79m
Draft: 4'6"/1.37m
Builder: Trumpy Boatyard,
Annapolis, Md.
Hull: Wood
Engines: 2 X 1271N Detroit Diesels
Year: 1962

Dreamboat was built in 1962 at the Trumpy boatyard in Annapolis, Maryland for John Kimberly of Kimberly-Clark. Originally called *Eskimo*, the yacht was built primarily for speed and it's been said that she has pulled waterskiers behind her. The succession of owners after Kimberly were Louis Wolfson of Wometco Enterprises, James Ryder of the trucking family, Bernie Little of Anheuser Busch, and Frank Loving, collector of antique boats who finally sold this prized Trumpy to the present owners, Spencer Boat Co. The boat has had as many names as owners.

Ed Bronstien, Jr., president of Spencer Boat Co. in West Palm Beach, Florida, and his son Jim who works with him, have made a special project out of restoring the ageing Trumpy. Being in the business of servicing, refurbishing, and repairing all types of yachts, the Bronstiens have taken particular care to make *Dreamboat* their "Showboat."

Michael Parenti of Omni Interiors, North Palm Beach, orchestrated the interior design and renovation. An attempt to preserve the original boat was the goal. Wood that had been painted over was stripped and refinished to the natural grain. Parquet flooring and Trumpy furniture were also restored. The main salon is flanked by large picture windows. The aft deck is similarly a comfortable place to lounge, protected but not removed from the great outdoors. *Dreamboat* has three staterooms and heads in the aft section. With such a narrow hull, the sleeping accommodations were rather limited. However, Spencers altered all of the bunks to allow for more space. They also increased the fuel and water tank storage so that fuel tanks for 2,000 gallons can carry the boat 1,000 miles.

The boat is used for entertaining, and a party of about one hundred is not unusual. *Dreamboat* was the lead boat in the annual Palm Beach and Ft. Lauderdale Christmas parade in December 1985. With all of the superduper new and modern yachts in the parades, the old Trumpy still turned a lot of heads.

Empress Subaru

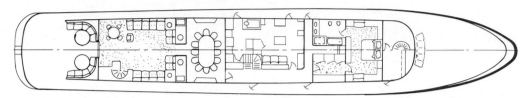

Type: Flybridge Motor Yacht with dual
 controls
LOA: 154'/47m
LWL: 140'/42.7m
Beam: 2 5'/7.6m
Draft: 12'3"/3.7m
Builder: C.R.N., Ancona, Italy
Year: 1979-82
Hull: Steel
Engine: Twin MTU/2250 hp each
Cruising: 14knots @ 1100 rpm

Empress Subaru belongs to the Subaru Distributors in Orangeburg, New York, so of course there is a Subaru car sitting on the aft bridge deck. Keeping company with the automobile is a 25-foot Boston Whaler and a Bell Jet Ranger helicopter. Forward on the bridge deck is the helm station. There is a centerline console with complete electronics and twin leather observation seats port and starboard. A radio room and ship's office with the captain's cabin is opposite. Aft of this area is a stately office/lounge with a wet bar and powder-room. Smoked glass doors lead out to the deck.

On the main deck all the way forward is the owners' stateroom. There are numerous portholes which add a lot of light to the cabin. The king-size bed is in the middle of the room, built into a teak frame that blends handsomely with the wood panelling. To port is a large bathroom, complete with tub, shower, double sinks, bidet and w.c. The entrance to this stateroom is through a passageway on the starboard side with a dressing room, deck and sitting area. Next aft is a well-designed and practical galley. A fair amount of entertaining is done onboard so the chef is often called upon for imaginative food preparation.

The dining area aft of the galley seats eight, and the main salon, with its peach colored silk couches, comfortably accommodates at least fifteen. The walls are panelled in beautiful woods with louvered shutters the length of the salon. Well chosen art work enhances the space. There is nothing overdone on this yacht; she is subtle and serenely appointed. Aft of the main deck are two circular lounge areas built in with two pedastal tables. There are private conversation corners in several areas both inside and out.

The lower deck houses the crew and the guest staterooms. The largest of the guest staterooms has a double bed, ensuite bathroom, and its own sauna. There are twin staterooms with twin beds and private baths. Aft of these staterooms is the engine room and machine space, and aft of that are still more guest accommodations. The yacht sleeps twelve in the owners' party and eleven in the crew.

Empress Subaru is designed similarly to many of the great sailing yachts, with lots of wood, rounded edges, and an eye toward functional aesthetics.

J.J. L'HERITIER

J.J. L'HERITIER

J.J. L'HERITIER

J.J L'HERITIER

Felicita

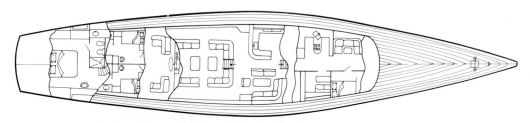

Type: Sailing Yacht
Length: 128'/39m
LWL: 92'/28m
Beam: 25'/7.6m
Draft: CBD/19'/5.79m
CBU/7'6"/2.30m
Displacement: 200 tons
Builder: Perini Navi, Viareggio, Italy
Designer: Dick Carter
Hull: Steel
Engines: 2 GM8V71 350 HP each
Sail Area: 550 sq. meters

Felicita is a radical departure from the traditional sailing yacht. Built by Perini Navi in Viareggio, Italy, the boat is basically a Dick Carter design. However, entrepreneur, builder and inventor, Fabio Perini has certainly exerted his influence. *Felicita* incorporates the comfort, liveability, and technology of a motor yacht with the beauty, motion and fascination of a sailboat. The modern retractable keel, useful in ports and shallow waters, can be extended for better performance upwind, retracted for less wetted surface downwind. The rig is totally unconventional in that the loose footed sails are operated electronically. In fact, just about everything can be operated from the pilot-house electronically, allowing this 120-foot yacht to be sailed easily and efficiently by only two or three people. The boat is also fitted with an innovative self-furling system to make it easy to reduce sail canvas under sail. There are twin self-furling jibs. Unusual and effective is the full-fledged flying bridge with external and internal controls. While the flying bridge and small sundeck make the boat look modern, the hull has a traditional stern with a significant overhang and the sheer is well defined.

The accommodations are smart and elegant, but hardly conventional. Aft on deck is a large open-air salon, sheltered by the superstructure, with U-shaped settee and dinette. The main salon is open and resplendent in a rich brown leather. The leather couch extends forever, it seems, forming a complete squared off circle around two coffee tables. About thirty people can be seated. Forward of the main salon is a dinette area to starboard and a serving bar to port. The serving bar has an interesting refrigerator with a stainless steel panel that has bottle-sized holes in it to secure bottles when the refrigerator is opened. A refrigerated glass cabinet is customized for individual hand blown signed glasses. There is also a sink, icemaker, and espresso machine. Wrap around windows insure that the salon is in direct contact with the outside world.

Below decks, the sleeping quarters are separated into three distinct areas, each with independent access. The full beam owners' stateroom is aft. It boasts a king-size bed, ensuite bathroom and a small office. The central zone has four guest cabins, each with its own bathroom. Two have single beds and two have double beds. The wall between the double bedded state rooms is

able to recess into the bulkhead creating one large suite if desired. Each cabin has its own self contained entertainment center, including a built-in stereo, T.V. and V.C.R.

The galley, pantry, skipper's and crew's quarters are all forward. The crew on *Felicita* enjoy a particularly pleasant dining area which is spacious and has a leather upholstered settee. They too have their own entertainment center. The radio room is replete with all of the latest navigational equipment as well as a comfortable desk and settee area.

The galley is exceptionally well organized with a center stove and work counter. The refrigerator has stainless steel drawers to keep different items at proper temperatures. These drawers also make it unnecessary to open the whole refrigerator in search for a particular item. There is plenty of ventillation in the amidships galley.

Felicita is designed for comfort and speed. With the spirit of the 'round the world cruiser, Viareggio based Perini Navi makes its entry into the exclusive glamorous club of large boat builders.

Felicita

Golden Eagle

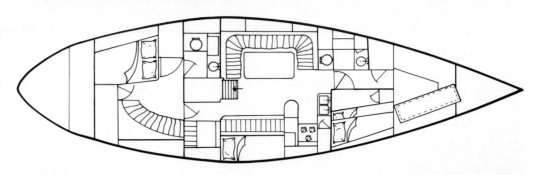

Golden Eagle was built as a racer/cruiser by Sparkman & Stephens for the competitive sailor who never wants to see a pipe berth again. Her pedigree and ability have been proven by victories over all-out Grand Prix IOR racers. Her decks have been arranged with simplicity and forethought, all equipment is top quality: self tailing Barient winches, Harken hardware, Sparcraft spars, Doyle racing sails. Still when you go below, the living space and beauty have not been sacrificed.

The bulkheads and the dining table are crafted out of bird's eye maple. The light colored wood is accented by mahogany. Red velvet upholstery adds an elegant touch and a warm welcome after a hard day of working the coffee grinder. Berthing arrangements include a large double cabin with head aft, a private double cabin forward, three berths in the main salon and one in the fo'c'sle.

Racing sailors may never want to rough it again.

Type: Offshore Racer/Cruiser
LOA: 52'/15.85m
LWL: 42'/12.80m
Beam: 15'6"/4.72m
Draft: 9'2"/2.79m
Designer: Sparkman & Stephens
Builder: Eric Goetz Custom Sailboats
Engine: 70hp Westerbeke Diesel
Cruising speed: 7.5 knots
Year: 1983
Hull: Wood with Nomex core

Gran-Mudder

THE BROCHURE PEOPLE, FT. LAUDERDALE, FL.

Gran-Mudder is a one of a kind vessel built at the Mei Shipyard, Yokaichi, Japan in 1980. The original owner was an Arabian sheikh; however, Texans Mr. and Mrs. John Mecom purchased her and thoroughly redesigned her in 1983. They worked in coordination with Italian designer Giorgio Vafiadis. The result is a spacious environment that acts as a backdrop for the Mecom's extensive art collection. There is a distinctive Art Deco flair to the decor, particularly with the accent pieces: Edgar Brandt and Tiffany lamps, tables, sculptures, and panels.

The main salon is dedicated to a large entertaining area which spans the full width of the yacht. Two distinct seating arrangements of custom-made sofas, upholstered in pearlized leather and suede, provide an opportunity for intimate conversation. The plush white carpet and soft leathers are a textural complement to the high-gloss burlwood. Invisible neon lights, recessed on the lower part of the ceiling create an illusion of height. The central part of the ceiling is gray suede.

Large windows in every direction frame a panoramic view. The focal point of the main salon is the half-circle bar upholstered with alligator skins.

A short passage connects the main salon with the dining room where a smoked mirror-covered wall lends a foggy reflection of the outside world. A black solid handrail finished in mother of pearl assists the inexperienced passenger when the sea gets a bit rough.

The dining salon has special lights, recessed in the black lacquer ceiling, to enhance the drama of the Art Deco design. Dark gray mirrors on the central ceiling dramatize the mother-of pearl walls. Comfortable leather chairs, seating twelve guests, draw up to a travertine dining table.

The two principal staterooms, one forward on the main deck, another below deck, extend the full width of the yacht and include sitting rooms and large private baths ensuite. Each has a king-size bed and burlwood cabinetry, trimmed with brass.

In addition to the principal staterooms, there are four double guest rooms on the lower deck. Different colors distinguish the rooms. There is the black and ivory room (the only one of the guest rooms with a double bed), the blue and white room, the gray and pink room, and the light blue and gray room. The yacht is frequently seen in the Caribbean.

Type: Motor Yacht
LOA: 151'/46m
Beam: 26'/7.9m
Draft: 8'6"/2.59m
Builder: Mei Shipyard, Yokaichi, Japan
Year: 1980
Hull: Steel
Engines: Twin MTU main engines, 1100 hp
Speed: 14 knots cruising

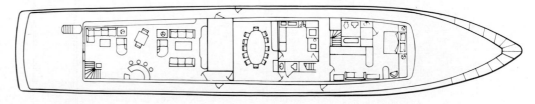

The objectives of designing *Gran-Mudder* were threefold: 1. To improve any features that would enhance the quality of life on the yacht, thereby creating a more pleasant, relaxing, and comfortable environment; 2. To integrate the joy of entertaining with the intimacy of a private conversation and fine dining; and 3. To upgrade the yacht to reflect the current owner's taste and lifestyle.

My intention was to create an environment that was unique and decidedly different from the other yachts previously owned by the Mecoms. To this end, the use of traditional woods, so characteristic to most yachts, was excluded.

Life on the sea can be full of adventure. Before a storm, there is a moment of extreme quiet and stillness as the water loses its warm, emerald-blue color and the sky turns gray. It is this very shade of gray that we chose as the master color for the living areas, incorporated into the selected materials and finishes and complementary color schemes. Various shades of blue, the Mecom's blue, harmonize the interior with its natural surroundings.

To design a yacht is not easy. There are limits as to what can be done and how it is to be done. There are high standards to meet. Using technology, know-how, and ingenuity, we minimized the limits and created an inspiring, safe, comfortable and functional living environment.

Giorgio Vafiadis

Hetairos

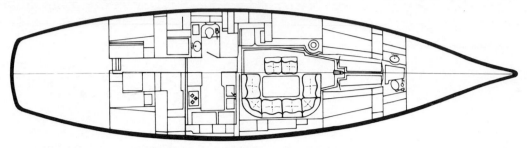

Hetairos was designed by Henry Scheel, with lines in the classic yankee tradition of L. Francis Herreshoff's *Ticonderoga*. She has a rakish clipper bow, hollow waterline forward and a beautiful heart-shaped transom aft. Her deckline, raised bulwarks aft, silver dolphins, varnished caprails, and hatches lead one to believe that the vessel was built and designed in the 1930s. She was, in fact, built at the Royal Huisman Shipyard in Holland in 1985.

The German owner of *Hetairos* originally wanted a yacht similar to a Swan 65, because he thought that type of racing yacht would yield him the performance he was looking for. He found that he could combine the aesthetics he was interested in with performance. *Hetairos* was designed with a modified fin, which is Scheel's keel and rudder. This makes for a fast modern underbody with a long waterline. The Scheel's keel makes her quite stiff, shoal, and weatherly. All of the interior joinerwork is executed in sandwiched covered foam veneer, which has kept the weight extremely light.

Her powerful rig is completely hydraulic roller furling, built by Rondal. It allows two people to take this boat out. With the complete Lewmar hydraulic winch package she is extremely easy to operate. She has a complete complement of electronics which include the Scanti receiver, telex, weather chart, and AP satellite navigator and complete Brookes and Gatehouse sailing instruments.

The accommodation includes an owners' stateroom aft, with main salon, galley, and head, sensibly placed in the center of the vessel just over her center of gravity. *Hetairos* is the 1980s version of a "proper yacht."

Type: Ketch
LOA: 65′7″/19.99m
LWL: 53′/16.15m
Beam: 15′/4.60m
Draft: 8′/2.45m
Displacement: 36 tons
Designer: Henry Scheel
Builder: The Royal Huisman Shipyard
Year: 1985
Hull: Aluminum

Highlander

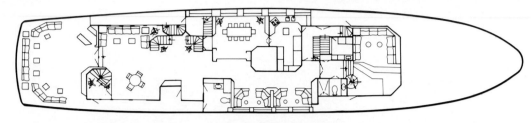

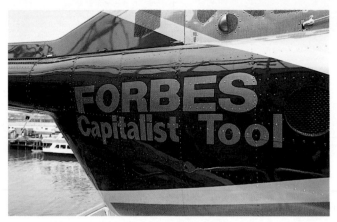

Type:	Motor Yacht
LOA:	150'11'/46m
Beam:	29'3''/8.91m
Draft:	9'9''/2.97m
Displacement:	447 tons
Designer:	Jon Bannenberg
Builder:	De Vries Shipyard
Year:	1985
Hull:	Steel
Engines:	2 GMC 16V149, 900 hp each @ 1800 rpm
Cruising speed:	13.7 knots
Max. speed:	14.3 knots
Fuel cap.:	19,700 gallons Range: 3,000 nautical miles, 5,300 gallons

Highlander number 5 is the latest of Malcolm Forbes' yachts. Highlander number 1 in 1955 was a 78-foot converted Canadian Corvette. Then came the 98-foot Feadship launched in 1957, followed by the 117-foot vessel which burned down a few years ago. A 126-foot Feadship became the interim yacht while the new *Highlander*, pictured here, underwent design and construction.

The yacht was built at the big de Vries yard in Aalsmeer, not far from Amsterdam. Frits de Voogt, the naval architect, known as the father of Feadship, is responsible for engineering and hull design, and Jon Bannenberg orchestrated styling and the interior.

The new *Highlander*, like her predecessors, is especially designed for corporate entertaining in which her owner, Malcolm Forbes, frequently indulges. The launching of the gigantic green boat was like a theatrical production, complete with a huge audience and bagpipes. Forbes and family arrived in his Boeing 727, the "Capitalist Tool," to witness the launching after which the first supper was held aboard: a dinner party for a mere eighty. Apparently, even from day one, the yacht was a huge success.

Some people think it strange that Malcolm Forbes would have such an unconventional yacht. However, the man who flew a hot air balloon across America and who made the first motorcycle tour of China certainly is not lacking in imagination. *Highlander* resembles the revolutionary design of *Azteca*, but the interior arrangement is quite different. Forbes often conducts business on his yacht and he likes to ensure that his guests are treated royally. To this end, there are six distinctive salons for guests. Bannenberg has totally altered all of the conventions of traditional interior yacht design by disregarding the concept of the yacht as a linear structure. "On a linear structure you have a central corridor and things port and starboard. This automatically halves all of the space and causes terrible traffic problems," says Bannenberg. On the *Highlander*, the corridors or "throughways" are offset to allow people to flow freely from one end of the boat to the other.

The multitudinous salons are simply decorated. Walls are either panelled in birds-eye maple or are lacquered, floors are teak and holly, ceilings are covered in gray padded leather, and carpets are gray. Marble is everywhere in five different colors. Sofas and banquettes are upholstered in subtle quiet tones. The neutral coloring is the perfect background for many of Forbes's collectibles which are on display, including three Art Deco panels from the liner *Normandie*, wooden columns and stained glass from the Royal Yacht *Victoria and Albert*, which decorate the twelve-seat dining salon, nautical dioramas displayed in plexiglass coffee tables, artworks by Cocteau, Dufy, and Gainsborough, and a host of personal memorabilia.

The amidships salon has access to the observation room. The stairs going to this room have peach lights glowing beneath each step. The deck dining room provides additional area for entertaining, and then on top of it all is a kind of crow's nest around the mast which allows for a spectacular view.

The green master stateroom and the four color coded guest staterooms are belowdecks. Lucite handrails are conveniently situated on staircases that descend to the five staterooms. Mr. Forbes's suite sited aft, features a stern window and seating alcove like sailing ships of old. His bathroom features a double sized whirlpool bathtub and vivid green marble steam room.

Six crew staterooms are near the machinery and operational end of the yacht. The wheelhouse is a multipurpose communications center. There are a staff of thirteen aboard *Highlander*. Truly the complete yacht with all the accoutrements; a pair of speedboats, a couple of Harley Davidsons, and a Bell Jet Ranger helicopter. Wasn't it Malcolm Forbes who said that the only difference between men and boys was the price of their toys?

Highlander

Management and control are essential components in design because of the complexity and sophistication of today's yachts. Each design poses a new set of conditions to be met. I have always been interested in design geometry and the exterior of a yacht is essentially a three-dimensional sculpture. The hull must vary according to the speed, performance, and intention.

The superstructure must relate to that hull form, reflect the space it encloses, but at the same time form a concordant bond with all the elements of the external appearance of the yacht. For me, an additional fascination is that the external skin encloses a form in which space must be divided and surfaces must be dealt with in a harmonious way. Perhaps, my training as a concert pianist enables me to envision architecture as frozen music.

Since harmony is the essence of yacht design, the inter-relationship of external shapes, the internal volume, plus the treatment of the two is of paramount importance. As all boats are in essence fore and aft longitudinal shapes, one is playing a type of three-dimensional chess to relating spaces within that form vertically, horitonzally, and athwartships in order to create spaces with the minimum number of longitudinal corridors.

At the same time the internal spaces must have access to the view through the windows. The windows themselves must relate to disparate factors and each other regarding the external appearance of the yacht. Thus the interior and the exterior of the yacht are indivisible.

No matter how small some spaces inevitably become, one must always bear in mind that the human form does not reduce in volume when it steps aboard a boat. There is no logic in reducing the size of door handles, fittings, chairs, closets, or cupboards. Despite the restrictions of a self contained space, shoreside requirements still apply on board a yacht.

New construction techniques and new materials are always a creative challenge. Each material; glass fibre, wood, metal, or carbon fibre, must be used in its own way and its own sympathetic use. I like to adapt my designs to suit the inherent nature of the material.

Each yacht I design is as different as each client. Therefore, I have the challenge and the pleasure of resolving the same problem in a multitude of distinctive ways. It is inevitable that I have a strong connection to my clients. After all, when you spend eighteen months to two years trying to express and understand a client's lifestyle, a close rapport develops.

Yachts are extremely complex constructions, something equivalent to a hand-built jumbo jet. Therefore the amount of input from talented people is significant. The essential solution is the integration of all the people and factors into a collective, organized whole. I am fortunate to have a terrific team working with me. We listen to our clients and transform their concepts into a finished reality which includes sketches, samples, detailed plans and models. I don't like to leave anything to the imagination. That is; I believe in considering every minute detail. During a recent interview for *The Yacht Magazine,* mention was made of my "snail tong list." This list has become a metaphor for the thoroughness with which I complete a yacht.

I'll never forget my embarrassment when a new owner had escargots on the very first menu, and the steward could not find the tongs for lifting the snails out of their hot shells. We then added them to the outfitting list along with monogrammed table napkins, salt cellars, and garlic squeezers. When we hand over a boat, I like the owner to step aboard with his guests and sail right away, with everything in its proper place. From the very first day both the owner and the yacht commence a life together. I like to think that we tailored the yacht to fit that life. I consider it a great privilege to be able to make dreams take shape.

Jon Bannenberg

ALAIN GUILLOU

Huaso

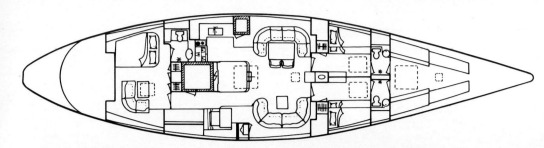

Type: Sloop rigged maxi racer/cruiser
LOA: 81'/24.7m
LWL: 68'2''/20.80m
Beam: 20'/6.10m
Draft: 13'6"/4.1m
Displacement: 38 tons
Ballast: 18.7 tons
Designer: German Frers
Builder: The Royal Huisman Shipyard, Holland
Interior Designer: Pieter Beeldsnijder
Year: 1984
Hull: Aluminum

*H*uaso is a unique vessel. She was built for a Spaniard who had a desire to race and cruise. She is a Maxi boat, measuring 81 feet overall. She was designed by German Frers and built and launched by the Royal Huisman Shipyard in the spring of l984.

Huaso's interior was outrageously appointed with special materials such as leather and alligator skin. Furthermore, the entire interior was modular built so that it could be removed. She can change from a fully comfortable cruiser to a stripped down Maxi interior in a matter of hours. A container, in which the interior modules are stored during racing periods, was designed to travel with the boat. Eight hours after the races are over, the boat can again be ready to cruise.

Huaso was used for her first year by her owner in the Mediterranean mainly as a cruising vessel. In 1985, she sailed to the Caribbean where she cruised from the Grenadines to Antigua. Afterwards, she came up to race the Southern Circuit and had the interior removed. She raced the Southern Ocean Racing Circuit against *Kialoa*, *Boomerang*, and *Condor*. She gave a very good account of herself, winning two races and the series. Shortly after the series, her owner decided to have a new boat built, which emphasized cruising, and he sold the yacht to Mr. Bill Koch, who changed her name to *Matador*. She then went to the Robert E. Derecktor yard and was converted to a full-out racing machine and is considered one of the premier Maxi boats on the racing circuit today.

KO WELLEMAN

THEO KAMPA

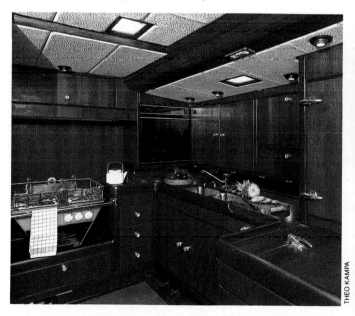

THEO KAMPA

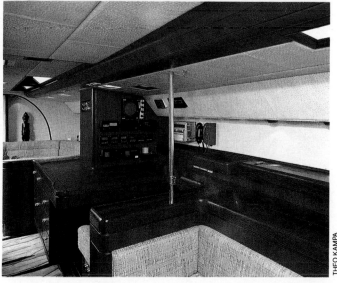

THEO KAMPA

Infinity

JOHN WISDOM

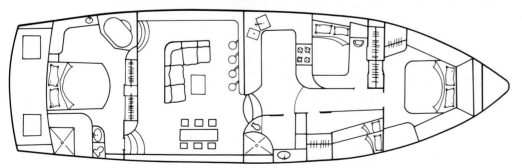

Type: High Speed Motor Cruiser
LOA: 66'8"/20.3m
LWL: 57'5"/17.50m
Beam: 20'10"/6.35m
Draft: 3'6"/1.06m
Displacement: 40,000 lbs.
Designer: Harry Schoell
Builder: Infinity Yachts/Nautical
   Engineering Corp.
Year: 1984
Hull: Delta Conic
Engines: 2 GM 6-71TI Diesels
Max. Speed: 24 knots

JOHN WISDOM

nfinity is a 67-foot motor yacht with a displacement of only 32,000 lbs., about half the weight of a normal fiberglass cruiser of the same size. She is a prototype for a revolutionary series of motor yachts designed by Floridian, Harry Schoell who has patented a hull construction technique called the Delta Conic. What is unusual about this hull is that there is no mold; the hull is developed from flat sheets of materials (in this case they are prelaminated under vacuum) of vinylester resin and unidirectional fiberglass on each side of a balsa core. The bulkheads and stringers are similarly formed and the hull is bonded together much as a giant model kit would be. With this technique any size or shape of boat can be produced economically. Also, there are no underwater metal parts and little metal elsewhere. *Infinity* is light, relatively inexpensive to operate, and has very few problems with galvanic action.

Most striking about her appearance is the wishbone mast that supports a 644-square-foot roller furling, double luff sail that opens to 1,288 square feet off the wind. The mast can be raised and lowered via electronic winches. When lowered it forms a bulwark on the forward deck. The 14-foot tender is cleverly stored in a compartment just inboard of the transom platform. The platform also has a shower and there is direct access to the shower/dressing room in the aft cabin so swimmers fresh from the sea can pass through without dripping on the carpeted floor. The aft cabin also has a Jacuzzi.

All of the accommodations are commodious. The main salon features a lounging and a dining area as well as a breakfast bar. The barstools are ingeniously attached to stationary pipes and are constructed so that they can swivel from side to side, yet are fixed in place and need not be stowed under weigh. Forward of the bar and recessed to a lower level is the large galley. Additional staterooms to starboard and forward offer plenty of room for family or guests.

With a host of other yacht designs to his credit, Harry Schoell maintains *Infinity* for personal use, but he is constantly at the drawing board inventing new materials and methods of yacht construction and infinite creative devices to increase the pleasure in boating.

Jamaica Bay

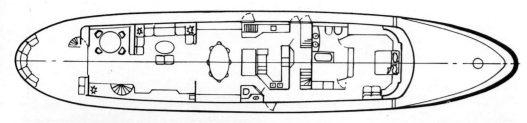

Jamaica Bay represents the ideal marriage of the old and the new. Built by Amels B.V., Holland, and designed by Diana Yacht Design in 1984, the structure, the engineering, the mechanics and navigational equipment are all state of the art. However, the interior is done in the classical style; mahogany panelling in the main salon takes you back to the turn of the century. A clean ship shape nautical theme with traditional colors, blue carpeting, and blue accent pillows on a white couch. There are nineteenth-century paintings from the Dutch school on the walls, and two oil paintings of sailing ships by Summer Scales.

The dining room is graced by a Sheraton table that seats ten. Royal Copenhagen China, fine silverware and crystal provide a touch of elegance. The boat deck features a library and lounge area. From the exquisite leather topped desk you can compose poetry whilst contemplating the sea, or you can keep abreast of what is happening at the office, for all of the latest instruments of communication are available from the navigation station adjacent to the lounge. The commodious captain's quarters are also on the boat deck aft of the bridge. The crew's quarters and the twin guest staterooms are on the lower deck. The two twin berth cabins have ensuite shower and w.c. They are furnished in a simple manner, with built-in beds and side tables out of mahogany and brass reading lamps—straight forward and classic.

The master stateroom and aft stateroom have king-size beds, bathrooms with bathtubs as well as television, video, and stereo cassette systems.

The aft deck and boat deck provide plenty of space for outdoor entertainment and the top sundeck can be transformed into a sea of cushions for private lounging.

Jamaica Bay is the answer for charter groups who want a little old world charm without sacrificing the comforts that the new vessel has to offer.

Type: Motor Yacht
LOA: 137′5″/42m
Beam: 26′3″/8m
Draft: 8′9″/2.7m
Tonnage: 429.57 gross/292.11 net
Builder: Amels B.V., Holland
Year: 1984
Hull: Steel (aluminum superstructure)
Engine: 2 X 850hp caterpillar diesel D 398T
Max. Speed: 14 knots
Cruising Speed: 12 knots
Fuel Capacity: 50,000 liters

KO WELLEMAN

KO WELLEMAN

KO WELLEMAN

Jessica

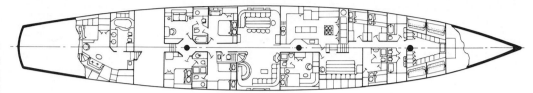

Jessica, the three-masted topsail schooner leaves you absolutely speechless. She is the dream vessel of Argentinean businessman, Carlos Perdoma. Reminiscent of turn-of-the-century schooners, she is both elegant and fast. Perdoma has owned a vast assortment of yachts including a 42-foot ketch, *Sonja,* a 40-foot S & S yawl, *Barracuda,* a 64-foot Frers, *Juana,* and *La Cautiva,* a 73-foot yawl with Herreshoff lines, and the famous schooner replica, *America .* He began thinking about building *Jessica* in 1979. At that time he had met and was impressed by Arthur Holgate who had built a 93-foot topsail schooner in South Africa, and had singlehanded from South Africa to St. Thomas.

Conceived by Perdoma, *Jessica* was planned in cooperation with Holgate and Perdoma's skipper, John Barden. She is a light displacement steel hull with a schooner sail plan, that can reach hull speed in 20 knots apparent wind. *Jessica* is the primary home of Carlos and his wife, Norma Jessica (the name of the yacht is derived from his wife's middle name). Perdoma wanted a fast, comfortable oceangoing yacht that would reflect the golden age of yachting. *Jessica's* design embraces style and class without being dogmatically attached to the old way of doing things. Simplicity and ease are of paramount importance. You can set the mizzen, main and foresails in 4 1/2 minutes due to the efficient power winches. Also, it is interesting to note that systems and parts are standardized. For instance the booms and gaffs are all interchangeable as are the top masts, many of the sails, and even the dorade vents.

Holgate designed the hull lines and the sail plan which were later checked and modified by Dutch naval architect Jan Coucke. The interior design was a cooperative effort of both Carlos and John Munford who worked for Camper & Nicholson for five years. *Jessica* was built at Astilleros de Mallorca S.A. in Palma. Spain's finest craftsmen spent three and a half years creating *Jessica.* Carlos and Norma lived near the boatyard and were totally involved in the yacht's creation.

Launched in 1984, *Jessica* sailed to Cowes where she was rigged and given engine and mechanical trials, then to the Caribbean, then back to the Mediterranean. Watching her accelerate under sail is truly a marvelous experience. She picks up speed rapidly and before you can get your camera out to photograph her she is far away on the horizon. The spacious sweep of her deck extends about half the length of a football field.

The interior is exquisite throughout. The master cabin has its own deckhouse, and is panelled in teak with a white overhead, large bed, built-in settee and vanity. There is even a small kitchenette for a private cup of tea. The owners' bathroom features an old fashioned bathtub with gold claw feet. The faucets on the twin ceramic sinks and on the bidet are also gold plated. Altogether there are four double cabins, each with an adjoining bathroom.

The main salon to starboard has an L-shaped green leather settee adjacent to a beautiful rounded bar. The bar is adorned with ivory tusks. In fact, ivory and scrimshaw are the dominating themes in both this room and the owners' study. Carlos is a hunter and collector of ivory and scrimshaw. Shelves which house his collections have been carefully planned so that all of the art objects stay put under sail. A magnificent gun collection is displayed in the library. Oriental rugs add warmth and beauty to all of the cabins.

Thirteen crew have their own quarters forward so that the owners and their guests have complete privacy.

The King of Spain, a friend of Carlos , gave him an eighteenth-century bronze bell as a launching present. Engraved with "Viento largo, mar calmo, y estrella clara"—a fair wind, a calm sea, and bright stars—what more perfect existence could anyone want?

Type: Topsail Schooner
LOA: 203'/61.8m
Beam: 28' 2"/8.6m
Draft: 12' 8"/4m
Displacement: 378 tons
Designer: Arthur Holgate
Builder: Astilleros de Mallorca
Year: 1983
Hull: Steel
Engine: GM 12V71 650 BHP @ 2300rpm
Max. Speed: 20 knots
Cruising Speed: 10.2 knots
Fuel Capacity: 30 tons

Jessica

Jezebel

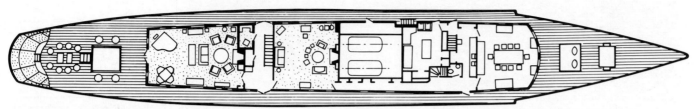

Type: Motor Yacht
LOA: 271'/82.6m
Beam: 34'/10.36m
Draft: 13'/3.96m
Tonnage: gross: 996/net: 298
Displacement: 1413 tons
Designer: Cox and Stevens
Builder: Freidrich Krupp Germania
  Werft A/G, Kiel, Germany
Year: 1930/major refit: 1983

GRAEME OUTERBRIDGE

Jezebel is perhaps the most exquisite restoration of a classic motor yacht afloat today. Designed by Cox and Stevens, and built in 1930 by Friedrich Germania Werf A/G Kiel, Germany, the yacht was commissioned by Mr. Algar of the Packard Car Company in the United States and was launched with the name *M.Y. Reveler*. However, in 1931, the yacht changed hands and was bought by Charles McCann, head of the Woolworth chain. He changed the name to *Chalena*, furnished her lavishly, and enjoyed her as a pleasure craft for over ten years.

Her fate changed drastically during the war years. In 1942, requisitioned by the U.S. Navy, she was converted to a gun boat by Gibbs Gas Engine Co., Jackson, Florida. The former pleasure yacht underwent a total metamorphosis. As the *USS Beaumont* PG60, she operated out of Pearl Harbor, carrying two 3-inch guns, 6 anti-aircraft guns, depth charges, and a crew of 110.

After the war, she underwent a major refit at the Bath Iron Works in Maine where her two 1100 horsepower Krupp engines were overhauled. In 1949 the yacht was renamed *M.Y. Elpetal* and became the property of Greek shipping magnate Marais Embiricos. The yacht remained in his family for twenty-six years during which time she was used for world cruising and the entertainment of many international celebrities.

Purchased in 1983 by Australian entrepreneur, Robert Stigwood, she was restored to her original state. The restoration included the distinctive clipper bow, spruce masts and teak decks. Modern equipment was installed: generators, watermakers, air conditioning, Vospers stabilizers, bow thrusters, a satellite communication system, radar, satellite navigation, and safety equipment. In the summer of 1985, the engines were totally rebuilt.

The interior is furnished in the manner of an elegant country house replete with antiques, Persian rugs, original paintings, and prints. The main salon is predominantly white and blue, with over stuffed couches and chairs and of course, a piano. The library is pine panelled with an open fireplace as the focal point. The dining room can elegantly accommodate twenty-four guests with the addition of two side tables. The galley with its stainless steel counters, two Vulcan stoves and center isle, is as efficient as any commercial kitchen.

87

Jezebel is capable of carrying a vast amount of provisions due to an enormous walk-in freezer and plenty of cold storage space.

The lower deck has seven guest staterooms named after Greek islands such as Petali, Spetsai, Andros, Syra, Tinos, Serifos, Miconos. The rooms are simple, with twin beds, and private bathrooms. The walls are painted in eggshell and the decor is subdued, usually white with one accent color, and of course, Persian rugs.

The master stateroom is on the boat deck, adjacent to a cozy little study. For the entertainment of the guests, there is a library of over 200 video films, a variety of television and stereo equipment, a sauna on the lower deck, and a Jacuzzi on the boat deck aft of the study.

The flavor of the early 1930s, an era of gracious living, of comfort, and simple elegance, pervades. What strikes one first on seeing *Jezebel* is that she is as graceful as any sailing vessel. Her lines are sleek, and her teak decks add to the ambiance of a sailboat. Yet, unlike a sailboat, she is spacious, light and airy. *Jezebel* embodies the traditional nautical elegance of the clipper ships.

Jezebel

sworn to secrecy as to the arrivals, departures, and destinations of the Burtons. It was on board *Kalizma* that Richard Burton presented Elizabeth with the million dollar blue-white 69.4-carat "Burton Diamond." One year, the Burtons went to England to make a film called *The V.I.P.'s*. Because of British quarantine laws, they were not able to bring their menagerie of cats and dogs on the airplane, so Elizabeth decided to sail *Kalizma* up the Thames and moor her in London. For the duration of the shooting, they lived on board with their animals. At other times, the yacht cruised the Mediterranean. Visitors to *Kalizma* ranged from royalty to film stars to politicians. When the Burtons parted, the yacht was sold.

Her next illustrious owner in 1982 was Peter de Savory, chairman of the Victory Syndicate, the British challenge to the America's Cup in 1983. *Kalizma* was used as the flagship for their twelve meter *Victory*, and served as a base for entertaining, meeting and living on board during the grueling trials leading up to the final competition.

After the America's Cup, she was sold to the current owners who ordered an extensive refit on her, including replacing her old diesel engine in 1985 with a M.A.N., 520 horsepower diesel still supported by twin Mercedes wing engines. Much updating of equipment and the interior took place at that time.

Created during the time of Edward VII, the accommodations include five double staterooms for owners and guests. A full width master stateroom (formerly Elizabeth Taylor's room) is on the main deck, and contains an oversized double bed, and at one time, an authentic Louis XV chaise covered in gold silk and a pair of 150-year-old Rococo mirrors. The adjoining master bath is furnished in white Italian tile with gold filigree.

The mahogany-panelled passageway from which all the rooms open, extends the length of the boat. The dining room features an exquisite L-shaped Chippendale table and a breakfront stores the elegant china service and the Waterford crystal. The main salon has a semicircular bar, panelled in teak. A double width floor-to-ceiling mahogany bookcase is used for additional storage. Four doors near the aft end of the salon can be folded back to open the aft deck.

Below decks, guest accommodations are divided into two areas, the forward area includes a second owners' suite (formerly Richard Burton's room), which contains a one hundred-year-old carved four-poster bed. Olive-gray filigreed tile complements all touches of antiquity. During the 1981-82 redecoration, the port guest stateroom was converted into a cozy panelled office/study with leather chairs.

Kalizma has had many lives, and has undergone many changes yet her aura and charm remain the same.

Kalizma

Lac II

TONY MORGAN

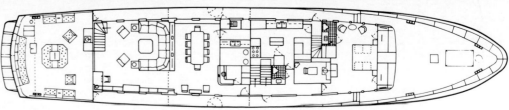

LAC II is invariably mentioned in the same breath as *LAC III,* and vice versa. Both yachts were commissioned and built by the late Roy Carver. Only one yacht was originally planned. Apparently Carver, unhappy with the progress of his yacht at the boatyard, Maritima de Axpe in Bilboa, Spain, decided to try the Feadship yard in Holland. *LAC II* from the Feadship yard was launched 18 months ahead of *LAC III,* in Spain. One of the yachts was earmarked for North America, the other for the Mediterranean. The unusual name was derived from Carver's mother's initials.

LAC II's hull was designed by Arthur de Fever of San Diego, California, and the interior was designed by Pierre Tanter who frequently makes use of decorative murals.

In 1976 the yacht was placed on the market and was sold almost immediately to Libya's Muammar Qaddafi, thus making up-to-date photographing impossible. Her name has been changed to *Hannibal* and Qaddafi has had her fitted out with electronic security systems including underwater sonic devices that monitor frogmen and such. The yacht is often kept in Malta, and is used primarily as a pleasure craft. The helicopter pad facilitates the comings and goings of Qaddafi and Co.

Type: Motor Yacht
LOA: 130'10"/39.87m
Beam: 25'7"/7.8m
Draft: 8'2"/2.49m
Builder: Feadship
Year: 1975
Hull: Steel
Engine: 2 Caterpillar Marine Diesel
  model D348 TA, 703hp @ 1800rpm
Cruising Speed: 14.7 Knots
Fuel Capacity: 13,450 U.S. gals./
  50,800 litres

Lars Porsena

Type: Express speed boat/buggy carrier
LOA: 42'10"/13.1m
Beam: 10'6"/3.2m
Draft: 1'9"/.54m
Displacement: 5.2 tons
Engines: 2 X 150 hp Volvo Penta AQD 40/280 Mercruiser 330 TR/ 2x 330
Builder: Tarquin Boat Company, England
Designer: Styling & interior/Terry Disdale

Lars Porsena is affectionately known as the "Buggy Carrier." Designed by Brit Terry Disdale for the Tarquin Boat Company, Ltd., this unusual yacht was intended as a luxurious, high-speed boat capable of being comfortable, and at the same time have the practical ability to carry sporting vehicles over considerable distances and land them on remote coast lines at will.

Lars Porsena is a combination of the world famous Rotork Sea Truck with GRP superstructure transformed into a futuristic and stylish machine. It's the ultimate for knocking about on a weekend, but the accommodations enable you to take as long a trip as any conventional yacht.

Mariella

MIKE MEADE

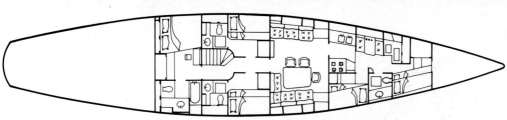

Type: Yawl
LOA: 79'/24.07m
Beam: 16'6"/5.03m
Draft: 11'6"/3.50m
Designer: Alfred Mylne
Builder: William Fife
Tonnage: 57 gross
Year: 1938
Hull: Wood

Mariella was built in Fairlie, Scotland in 1938 by William Fife and Sons for D. Paterson, a coffee importer. After the declaration of war, Paterson sold the boat to R.M. Teacher of the Scotch whisky family. Teacher retained her until 1969, at which time she was sold to a Mr. Pollok. She then had a series of owners until 1981 when she was purchased by Americans, Mr. and Mrs. Donald Glen who decided to restore her to her original state.

The restoration took place at the Porto Cervo S.A. Shipyard in Sardinia under the direction of the captain Ingmar Janum with the help of Malcolm Horsley (former skipper of the famous *Stormvogel*). Her teak decks remain original although the owners decided to have the deck house cut down to lower the profile of the boat. She is sleek and racy looking, with an interior that reflects the elegant '30s style. Her main salon is panelled in the original oak and the three cabins have been redone in teak. During the refit, the crew's quarters and the galley were both modernized.

Mariella is now run as a charter boat in the Caribbean. With the constant trade winds blowing, she can show off her superb sailing ability. She carries over 5500 square feet of sail and thrives in the conditions of the Windward Islands.It's fortunate that people recognize the beauty and craftsmanship of William Fife and other yacht builders of the golden age of yachting and are willing to preserve the heritage by rejuvenating these ageing beauties.

Mariette

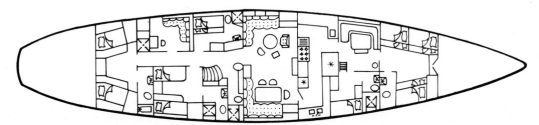

Type: Staysail schooner
LOA: 110'/33.55m
LWL: 89'9"/27.36m
Beam: 24'/7.32m
Draft: 15'/4.58m
Designer: Nathaniel Herreshoff
Builder: N. Herreshoff, Maine, U.S.A.
Year: 1918
Engines: 2 X GM 6-71 6 cylinder 185 hp diesels
Hull: Steel
Speed: 7 knots cruising; 8 knots maximum

Mariette, an exquisite 110-foot schooner, is typical of the elaborately outfitted schooners of the pre-World War I era. She was built by Herreshoff in 1915 in Bristol, R.I., for Bostonian Frederick Brown. She was later purchased by the Crowinshields. Mr. Crowinshield's ancestor was one of the first yacht owners in America and he had a vessel called *Cleopatra's Barge*. Crowinshield named his yacht *Mariette* after that notorious vessel that purportedly sailed across the Atlantic to help Napoleon depose the Pope. *Cleopatra's Barge II* remained in this family until 1939. She was requisitioned by the Coast Guard during World War II and used as a patrol boat. After the War she was sold again. Her third name became *GeeGee IV*. After changing hands a few times she was purchased by Canadian Walter Boudreau, and brought to the Caribbean. Boudreau changed her name to *Janeen* and operated her as a charter boat out of St. Lucia.

In 1979, Italian Alberto Rizzoli bought her and arranged to have her restored at the yard in La Spezia, Italy. The rebuilding under the technical direction of Erik Pascoli took place in 1981–82.

The teak decks are gloriously expansive with endless lounging space. There is a circular raised cockpit where guests can enjoy al fresco dining, or the table can be lowered to be used as a base for cushions.

Below decks one enters a bygone time of old world elegance. The companionway stairs are mahogany with carved bannisters and lead to a passageway and to a roomy main salon. On the port side is an L-shaped red leather settee around a coffee table facing an open fireplace. The original walnut panelling has been lovingly restored. A beautifully built-in walnut cabinet on the forward bulkhead holds some antique silver pieces and a few trophies that the yacht has won. On the starboard side is the dining table surrounded by red leather upholstered chairs and a settee.

The owners' stateroom is aft and has built-in berths port and starboard with a dresser between. The panelling in contrast to the walnut is light and there is a French provincial flavor to the room. The master head is painted a pristine white and the large bathtub and sink have mahogany trim.

Herreshoff built *Mariette* to sail, and sail she does. *Mariette* is often a winner in the sailing regattas that she enters. Over seventy years old and still young at heart!

Mariette

My Gail III

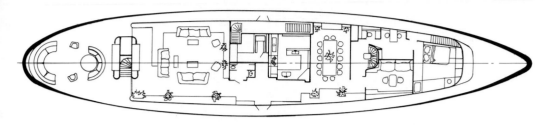

Type: Motor Yacht
LOA: 187'/57m
Beam: 29'6"/9m
Draft: 10'3"/3.1m
Designers: Jon Bannenberg/styling
and interior; Diana Yacht Design/hull
styling
Builder: Amels BV, Holland
Year: 1985
Hull: Steel
Engines: 3 98-KVA Volvo-Penta
gensets

JON BANNENBERG

JON BANNENBERG

My Gail III is quite spectacular. While Diana Yacht Design was contracted to produce the hull design and machinery layout, Jon Bannenberg is responsible for the exterior styling and the interior. The complex shapes and tight double curves were deftly constructed by the Amels Shipyard. Sophistication is the word that best describes *My Gail III*.

The main deck has a very large entertaining salon with some unusual features including a high tech hi-fi installation which plays in all areas, and which is controlled by infra-red remote control. The picture above the fireplace electronically moves to reveal a 26-inch television. A marble floored deck corridor leads to the dining room. The dining table is made of Baltic brown marble and has speakers and lights built into it. The owners' study, radio room, captain's cabin, captain's dinette/sitting area are all on this deck.

The top deck contains the owner's private salon which has four sofas around a coffee table. At the press of a button, the coffee table rises to the level of a dining table and the sofas track in to form a closed circular banquette underneath a skylight which displays a view of the mast above. Forward of this area across an oak parquet floor is the owner's cabin which extends the full width of the boat. There are large windows on both sides which add to the already spacious feeling of the room. Of course, there is the obligatory whirlpool double bathtub panelled with Azul Bahia marble.

Out from the top deck salon going aft is the boat deck and the port and starboard staircases leading to the owners' private sundeck. The sundeck has a large sunbathing mattress at the aft end and around the skylight (below which is the top deck salon).

The funnel contains a shower, bathroom, bar, and large storage room for the sunning mattresses when they are not in use. Sunken into one end of the funnel is a two meter diameter Jacuzzi bath positioned underneath the forward radar mast.

As opulent and indulgent as this yacht appears for the owner, she is nearly as luxurious for the crew. The lower deck which conventionally has the guest quarters aft has just the reverse on this boat, with crew's quarters aft. The crew on *My Gail III* can boast the best quarters of any yacht!

JON BANNENBERG

JON BANNENBERG

JON BANNENBERG

Nabila

Nabila ranks high among the most famous mega-yachts afloat today. She is owned by Saudi Arabian businessman, Adnan Khashoggi and is named for his beautiful daughter. The name means "noble" and the yacht certainly commands a regal presence no matter what harbor she is in. The exterior styled by Jon Bannenberg, with his trademark winged stacks, sleek long hull and bronze reflective windows, is modern and straight forward. The clean cut exterior belies an opulent interior.

The yacht, hardly a weekender's whim, is used extensively for business, living and entertainment. As the skipper says, "*Nabila* is not merely a yacht, she is a ship." She can and does travel worldwide. As an example of how seaworthy and how stable she is, the skipper enthusiastically recalls the terrific voyage to the Indian Ocean. The sophistication of the navigational systems and the electronic equipment can rival navy destroyers. The three clocks in the radio room relate the correct time in Riyadh, New York, and Rome, setting the tone for international business. With satellite communications, Khashoggi can, without sacrifice, maintain an effective central office. When the yacht is not in Porto Banus or Palma, she is quite possibly at her private berth in Antibes, docked a distance away from the rest of the world's fleet. Six telephone lines and approximately 280 telephones assure that no one aboard the yacht feels isolated. In fact, for being such a self-sufficient island, *Nabila* remains inextricably tied to civilization, as the mainland is only a helicopter flight away.

The yacht's interior was designed by Italian Luigi Sturcchio. As straight as the exterior is, the interior spaces are all curvacious circles, no sharp edges. The vast main salon has many cozy couch groupings, providing congenial conversation areas for many or for a few. On the same main deck level, is an intimate private dining room for family or small groups of friends. The bulk of entertaining, parties and dining is done on the upper deck which also includes the discotheque and aft deck lounge area.

The discotheque is comparable to any of the exclusive clubs in the major cities of the world. Midnight blue suede and gold lamé pillows lend a dressy look to the three circular couch arrangements. The floor is a mosaic of marble and metal and the ceiling is a high-gloss black lacquer accented by gold flecks.

There is a modular disc jockey stand with a plexiglass globe and a panel of buttons to make the room come alive with music and a light show. If the dancing gets too steamy, fresh air is accessible through doors to an aft deck lounge area.

For quieter entertainment, there is a small movie theater. Seven comfortable couches face the screen and there are plenty of cashmere blankets on hand to snuggle in with to watch your favorite feature. There is a movie library of over 1500 films.

The guest suites are so lovely and complete unto themselves that once you are settled in you may never want to leave. The staterooms are all named after precious and semi-precious stones or metals; the gold room, the silver room, and the sapphire, coral, lapis, diamond, ruby, emerald, and topaz suites. Each room carries out a color theme reminiscent of its namesake. The ruby suite with white lacquered walls and red curtains and candy striped couches combines a fanciful feminine motif with the coming of age. The bed has a curled upholstered head and foot rest, white lynx bedspread and satin pillows appliqued with red flowers. A dramatic red drapery hangs harem-like on either side of the bed. Above the bed is a circular mirror. A red and white pedastal holds a glass desk top and the TV, video stereo, entertainment unit is built into a red and white console facing the L-shaped couch. All of the walls are either panelled in white lacquered wood or in a soft leather. The bathroom of the ruby suite has pink flecked marble with an L-shaped bathtub, and cylindrical plexiglass shower with spray nozzles that spout from many directions.

Type: Motor Yacht
LOA: 281'9"/85.9m
LWL: 239'5"/73m
Beam: 43'3"/13.18m
Draft: 15'4"/4.67m
Displacement: 1,728 tons without helicopter
Exterior Design: Jon Bannenberg
Interior Design: Luigi Sturcchio
Builder: Benetti
Year: 1980
Hull: Steel
Engines: 2 Bofors 16 Cylinder 3000 bhp each
Speed: 17-18 knots

The emerald suite has green leathered panelling along with lacquered walls. The king-size bed is separated from a comfortable living area by the built-in entertainment unit (the TV can swivel to face both the bed and the couch.) Pushbuttons operate just about everything from the curtains and lights to the raising and lowering of the TV and the calling for the maid or valet service. The bathroom of the emerald suite has gold fixtures and green marble floors and counter tops. There are even his and hers green terry cloth bathrobes supplied to match the decor.

In addition to the numerous guest suites, there is a private wing for family which includes a private sundeck and small swimming pool. Also available onboard is a clinic and operating theater.

For fun at anchor, *Nabila* carries five powerboats, two Rivas, one Admiral, and two Boston Whalers.

There are so many details to take note of all around the boat. For instance, an entrance to an outside deck is designed so that the sliding doors open automatically à la James Bond. Speaking of which, the yacht *Nabila* played a bit part in the film, *Never Say Never*.

For a vessel that is in continuous use, *Nabila* is immaculately maintained, but of course she does carry fifty crew.

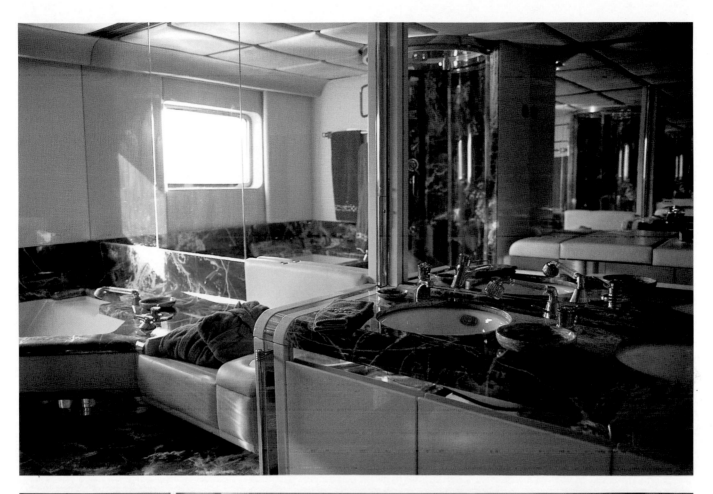

Nabila

Nabila

New Horizon L

Type: Motor Yacht
LOA: 197'/60.05m
Beam: 31'10''/9.70m
Draft: 13'/3.96m
Styling: Jon Bannenberg
Interior Design: Luigi Sturcchio
Builder: C. Van Lent & Zonen, Feadship
Naval Engineer: Frits de Voogt
Gross Tonnage: 889
Engine: 2 X MTU (Mercedes) 12 cylinder; 2 X 3000 hp
Year: 1983
Hull: Steel
Cruising speed: 15.4 knots
Max. speed: 18 knots

New Horizon L exudes opulence. She is the creation and the home of Prince Leon of Lignac, a Dutch businessman. The Prince is well acquainted with yachts, having owned a series of them over the years. Therefore, he wanted this yacht to be the culmination of his experience. To achieve the ultimate, he established a team of three top names in the yachting industry: Frits de Voogt, as naval architect, Jon Bannenberg as stylist and Luigi Sturcchio as the interior designer. *New Horizon L* was built at the Feadship yard at Van Lent & Zonen. The building of any megayacht is always a major production, but *New Horizon L* required an extraordinary feat of coordination. With Sturcchio as designer, much of the interior was fabricated piecemeal in small Italian workshops which specialized in fine woodwork, marble, oynx, and lacquerwork. The products created in these workshops had to be constructed in mock surroundings then disassembled piece by piece, wrapped in bubble plastic and transported to Holland. Container after container arrived at the Feadship yard, over 20,000 packages from around the world with items ranging from towel brackets to lacquer wall panels to marble bathtubs. The details, both functional and decorative on *New Horizon L*, are mind boggling.

Life aboard *New Horizon L* fulfills all fairytale notions about the royalty. Where else would you find a king-size Chinchilla bedspread, a round lapis lazuli bathtub, and 24-karat gold fixtures? The overall design concept of Luigi Sturcchio was to maintain simplicity and yet to use exceptional materials. Simplicity to Sturcchio apparently means white lacquered walls, ceilings of white goat leather trimmed in gold, polished mirrors and extensive marble. After all, gold-plated bannisters and columns are reminiscent of the brass nautical look of traditional yachts, but at least gold plating doesn't need daily polishing. To finish the total white background, Sturcchio designed carpets for every salon and suite so that the pattern would follow the lines of the furniture. The carpets were computer-woven in the United States at a width of thirty feet. The rolls were so enormous, weighing 14,000 kgs., that the ferry boat at Kaag had trouble delivering them. It took ten men to carry the rolls on board, and five carpet layers from Fields in New York to cut out of one piece of carpet the three suites, each with a hall and bathroom, and a corridor between them. The Prince takes great pride in these seamless carpets, while discussing how they provide color unity within the yacht.

Numerous showcases in the corridor, the dining room and in the suites display a wealth of art objects collected by the owners, many from the Orient. Particularly noticeable are the large Thai statues. The art objects and small statuary are all ornate, especially the elephant studded with emeralds, topaz, rubies, and other gems.

New Horizon L has five levels: the top is the helicopter pad and the sun deck. Even though there is a helicopter pad, there is no helicopter onboard. The owner feels that the disadvantages of a helicopter outweigh their advantages, so he simply rents one on occassion. The second is the entertainment deck with terrace, grand salon, bar and wheelhouse, the third is the main deck with two entrance halls, gallery, dining room, and owners' apartment; the fourth is the lower deck with second owners' suite aft, three guest staterooms, the engine room in the middle and staff and crew's quarters forward of it. The last level, seven feet high, holds the tanks and storage spaces.

The owners' apartment is at the end of a 62-foot corridor. The doors to this area are Korean, with mother-of-pearl inlaid dragons on the front. Through the doors is the owners' study. The desk faces a large picture window. Cleverly hidden in the desk drawers are a computer and typewriter. The floor-to-ceiling glassed-in bookshelf is used for art objects as well as books. Lapis lazuli accents the pedastal of the desk and cabinets in the study. Behind the desk is a reception lounge with a curved settee and a portrait of Leon of Lignac on the wall. The study leads into the master bedroom. On either side of the bed are lacquer panels inlaid with mother of pearl. Two Bhudda statues watch over the bed, perhaps to guard the incredible Chinchilla bedspread. The sprawing bathroom is incorporated into the bedroom. Lapis Lazuli is the theme. The tissue box and even the razor and toothbrush handles are lapis! A white marble fountain feeds the lapis bathtub. The gold-plated fixtures were designed by Sherle Wagner.

A gold bannistered staircase leads to the lower deck and the guest suites. The modern suite, black and white, has a bathroom where the tub is carved out of one piece of marble, which comes from Pakistan. The Japanese suite features gold tones and pale yellows and greens and of course artifacts from Japan. The Chinese suite has gold and gray-blue tones, and carries decor appropriate to the room's name. All of the suites have glassed-in showcases which carry countless treasures.

The second owners' suite decorated, in luscious peach and cream tones, is visually divided into three areas: a lounge nook, the sleeping area with king-size bed, lavishly covered in breathtaking white mink, and the bathroom, all white marble, accented by gold flecked marble and gold-plated fixtures.

The grand salon has a ceiling which is a mosaic of marble and mirrors. The two fountains are cut out of one block of marble. The comfortable down-filled couches are upholstered in white silk and two ottomans add contrast with their black and white patterned silk. There is a three-way view of the sea out of the large windows.

The grand salon opens to a deck dining area which is protected overhead and on the sides by plexiglass wind screens, so that outdoor living is possible in all weather. Beautifully carved sofas were built as part of the deck. The round dining table is marble and is surrounded by wicker chairs with pastel striped cushions. Above this table is a mirror set into the overhead which enhances a view of the sea. This is the least formal area on board.

There are twenty-seven full time crew on board, and the multitudinous stewards see to your every need. A guest on the *New Horizon L* is treated as if he is at the most first-class resort in the world. Every necessity is provided: lacquered boxes contain snacks, a liquor cabinet in every suite is available with set ups, bathrobes and slippers are laid out for you and all of your clothes are unpacked and ironed for you while you are sipping a welcome drink. Of course, full entertainment units are in each suite.

Run like a mini ship, (worldwide communications are accessible at all times) *New Horizon L* has everything. She even owns her own berth at Cannes (specially built for her, because of her size) and in Palma, and holds a long-term lease in Ft. Lauderdale. *New Horizon L* does go on extended cruises but the owner often stays on board, and enjoys only the passing scenery from the comfort of his own living room. Why leave?

New Horizon L

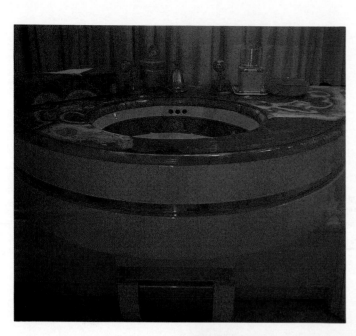

New Horizon L

New Horizon L

New Horizon L

Type: Motor Yacht
LOA: 110'/33.5m
Beam: 25'/7.6m
Draft: 7'6"/2.3m
Designer: Benetti Yachts
Builder: Lloyds Ships of Australia
Year: 1985
Hull: Steel
Engines: Twin MTU 8V396TB
82's/845hp each
Speed: 14 knots at 1650 rpm

Night Crossing is exemplary of a new trend in yacht design, one in which traditional nautical motifs are thoroughly discarded. Roy Sklarin, president of Star Designs and Yacht Sales, Ft. Lauderdale, is associated with Lloyds Ships Holding PTY Ltd., Brisbane, Australia, as their primary interior designer. Sklarin maintains *Night Crossing* as both his personal yacht and a showcase. Her name was taken from a movie and she is, in fact, a star. She was featured at the 1985 Ft. Lauderdale International Boat show as the premiere yacht and in the winter of 1986 she was used as a setting for the popular American television show, *Miami Vice*.

The interior of *Night Crossing* is a veritable floating piece of art. The colors black and cream have been fanatically used, accented with a stunning combination of etched glass, mirrors and anodized brass which does not tarnish. There is indirect lighting throughout and creamy silk wall coverings, silk plants and various objets d'art. The upper deck is accessed from a mirrored foyer on the main deck via a mirrored circular staircase. Black radial rubber is used as a floor covering. The pilothouse has a light gray leather console accented by black Awlgripped trim. A matching benchseat is located aft. There is terrific visibility here as well as all the latest navigational equipment.

Aft of the pilothouse is a small service galley with a dumb waiter that services it and the two other galleys on the boat. Aft of this section is the "sky lounge" featuring the theme colors of black and cream. The bar has brass inlay and an illuminated pillar at one end also trimmed in brass. Opposite is a cream colored sofa and glass coffee table. This lounge opens out to the boat deck where dining al fresco is an option. A sun deck above the boat deck is yet another space for entertaining or private sunning.

On the main deck all the way forward and the full width of the boat is the master stateroom, containing a king-size bed which is set into an acrylic free form structure behind which, the entire wall is mirrored and framed by lighted etched glass. On either side of the bed are brass and aluminum night tables. Opposite the bed is a built-in black cabinet which spans the complete wall containing ample storage and an entertainment center. The his and hers bathroom accessed from either side of the bed has beautiful rose colored marble.

Aft of the stateroom is another small service galley and dumb waiter connected to the main galley on the lower deck and the small galley on the upper deck.

The main salon/dining room measures nearly 33 feet by 20 feet. The ceiling is done in three levels, one each of cream mica, black mica, and anodized brass on aluminum and has square recessed tube lighting in each step. The forward bulkhead of the salon features a spectacular panorama of the New York skyline. This neon lit wall has three controls, one which can dim or shut off

the lighting of the sky, creating a sunset glow, the second which controls the light reflected through the windows of the buildings and the third which illuminates the Brooklyn Bridge in blue lights. Cruising beneath the Bridge is an exact replica of *Night Crossing* etched in the glass.

The dining salon has an etched glass table with an illuminated acrylic base. The living room area of the main salon features a large semi-circular modular type ribboned sofa of cream kid suede and is faced by another matching sofa on the other side, both created by Desede of Switzerland. In front of each are glass cantilevered cocktail tables. The windows are framed with soft black pleated shades. Off the main salon is the aft deck accessed through large sliding glass doors. The aft furniture is black wicker (of course) and has a wet bar for entertaining and access to the swim platform through the transom door.

Guest staterooms and crew's quarters are all located on the lower deck level.

Art Deco is the dominant flavor of *Night Crossing*. The entire yacht with the ubiquitous black and bisque is most certainly one of the most dramatic yachts afloat today.

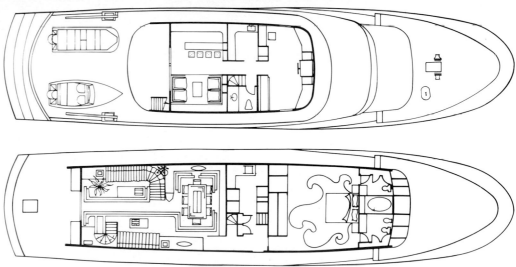

Nordwind

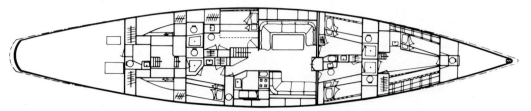

Type: Yawl
LOA: 85'6"/26.06m
LWL: 59'7"/18.20m
Beam: 17'/5.2m
Draft: 11'5"/3.48m
Builder: Burmester, Bremen-Burg, Germany
Hull: Wood
Year: 1938/39

Nordwind is a monument to prewar yacht design. In 1938, Donitz and Reeder, two admirals of the former German "Kriegsmarine" commissioned Burmester of Bremen-burg to build sister ships: *Nordwind* and *Ostwind*. The two yachts were built as the German challenge to all other ocean racers. They were intended as training vessels for the German Navy as well as for private use.

In 1939 *Nordwind* sailed her first and, until now, only Fastnet race. After a heroic race against the Fife *Latifa* she won the Elizabeth McCaw trophy for the first yacht around the Fastnet rock and the Erivale cup for the first yacht to finish. She set a record of three days, sixteen hours and twenty-eight minutes, which she held for twenty five years until 1965 when the record was broken by *Gitana IV*.

After the war both *Nordwind* and *Ostwind* were taken as prizes by Great Britain and the United States. Lord Astor then bought *Nordwind*. He took good care of her and sailed her until the 1960s, when he sold her. She fell into disrepair and ended up forgotten in a shed near Plymouth. It wasn't until 1976 that *Nordwind* again received attention. Two Dutchmen discovered her and purchased her for the price of the lead ballast in her keel. Then intensive restoration was started at the Camper & Nicholson repair yard in Gosport.

The entire mahogany planking below the waterline was replaced by two inches of iroko and sheathed with one millimeter copper plating as protection against worms and to prevent fouling. The wooden masts proved to be rotten and were replaced by aluminum spars. The project then lost momentum and work was halted as *Nordwind* was towed to Holland and laid up in Lemmer. In 1979, work began again. Under the direction of Jan Schoen, on behalf of the present owner (Northwind N.V., Willemstad, Curacao) total restoration and modernization occurred between 1981 and 1983. Gerard Dijkstra, the well known Dutch singlehanded yachtsman and designer, drew a new sail plan, deck and interior layout. Restoration of the hull including iroko planking above the waterline was completed during the winter of 1981/82 at the Bultjer yard in Ditzum on the Northsea coast of Germany. The only original parts of the hull that remain are the steel frames, the teak deck and the lead keel. Huisman of Vollenhove fitted the masts with new stainless steel rigging. In 1982 *Nordwind* returned to Enkhuizen in Holland for the completion of the work.

Nordwind is now a charterboat par excellence, operated with five crew. The main salon is panelled in beautifully varnished solid teak with cupboards and a glassed-in bookshelf over the dining area. The U-shaped settee is a luxurious chocolate brown leather as is the couch on the opposite side of the salon. The focal point as you descend the companionway is a magnificent built-in bar of matching teak. On either side of the bar are two oval doorways leading to two private double cabins, each with its own head. The galley to starboard of the amidships entrance is designed well for ocean sailing. The stove is gimballed athwartships and the cook would be protected well in a seaway. The dishes are all held into place by stainless steel pegs. Like the rest of the vessel every detail is carefully thought out with sailing and comfort in mind. There are two more guest cabins aft of the main salon, so that the boat can accommodate eight guests in addition to five crew.

The navigation station has its own private access from on deck. With his own space from which to read charts, the skipper need not be involved with the activities in the main salon.

Nordwind is truly a perfect yacht. Her lines are sleek, and she is fast. *Nordwind* has been resurrected in a first-class manner and is probably better than ever before.

Oceanfast 3000

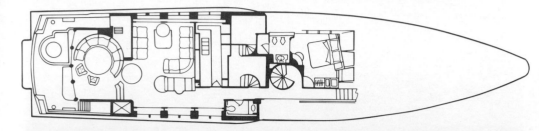

Type: Motor Yacht
LOA: 109'/33.3m
DWL: 95'/29m
Beam: 23'/6.98m
Draft: 5'10"/1.8m
Displacement: 60 tonnes (dry);
  80 tonnes (laden)
Designer: Styling/interior:
  Jon Bannenberg
Builder: Oceanfast, Australia
Hull: Aluminum
Year: 1985
Engines: 2 MTU diesels, 12 cylinder
  396T393 1960hp each
Cruising speed: 30 knots
Max. speed: 34 knots

Oceanfast 3000 was designed by Jon Bannenberg for the Perth shipbuilders, also called Oceanfast. This innovative production is affectionately called a "runabout." The profile of the yacht is radically futuristic, dominated by three picture window sized portholes. These oversized portholes add an interesting dimension to the interior of the boat, both aesthetically and luminescently. The main deck is multi-level and modular. Custom sculpted carpeting enhances the spatial flow. It is hard to believe that the interior is so curvaceous and soft when you see the sharp looking exterior.

The owners' stateroom is on the main deck and three guest staterooms and the crew's quarters are on the lower deck.

Most of Bannenberg's creations are seen in the Mediterranean and the Caribbean, but the revolutionary *Oceanfast 3000* is making the rounds of Perth, Adelaide, Sydney, and Brisbane. More yacht projects of this type are to follow in Australia, including a 43-meter flagship for the Royal Perth Yacht Club. Bannenberg feels there is a great future in large yacht building in Australia because of the lack of preconception of how things should be done.

COMPLIMENTS OF JON BANNENBERG

COMPLIMENTS OF JON BANNENBERG

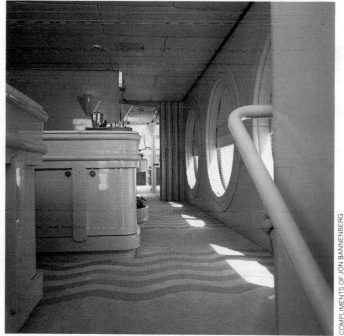

Orion

Orion was purportedly commissioned by the Royal Spanish family. However, her first owner was in fact a British Lt. Col. Courteney C. E. Morgan. The yacht was christened *Sulvana*. Following two British owners, she was bought by a Frenchman who changed her name to *Pays de France*. Her subsequent names were *Diane* and *Vera*. A Spaniard bequeathed her the name *Orion* in 1930. In all, *Orion* had twelve owners, five names, and flew five flags. In 1966 she was bought by a group of four Italians. She was dismasted en route from Barcelona to Marseilles. Her lovely panelled interior was painted white. In 1967 she was converted to a staysail schooner and her rig was shortened. Due to lack of attention, *Orion* fell into rapid disrepair. In 1970 she was decommissioned at La Spezia for four years and everything was removed from her, except the grand piano.

Two Italian brothers purchased her in 1978 and began major renovation that lasted two years. Now she is more beautiful than ever. The interior accommodations of *Orion* are exquisite. The deckhouse has mint green upholstered settees, an antique Persian rug, and a mahogany table and trim that are gleaming with care. An Austro-Hungarian silver champagne cooler is prominently displayed on the table. There is an arched window which allows access to the wheelhouse on the forward bulkhead of the deckhouse. The main salon is decorated with late eighteenth-century and early nineteenth-century furnishings. Persian rugs abound and original oil paintings do not look out of place. There is an eighteenth-century Venetian landscape attributed to Francesca Guardi over the fireplace, a Degas over the divan, and a seventeenth-century Jan Van der Meer is also in the main salon.

The dining table is set with Meissen china and Sheffield plates. The yacht's furniture is, for the most part, early nineteenth-century English. The panelling is a warm walnut. It is hard to believe someone could have painted over this lustrous wood.

There are accommodations for ten crew forward, a master stateroom aft, two cabins with double beds and two guest cabins with twin bunks. One of the heads has a bathtub that offers both fresh and salt water. It seems, back in 1946 when the Spanish Mata family owned the yacht, they were cruising with grandmother who loved bathing in the sea but was frightened of deep water. Hence, the installation of the third tap for salt water. There are, no doubt endless stories abounding on *Orion*, after so many years and so many owners. The present yacht is like a fairytale. She is big and beautiful and immaculately maintained. Once on board one is cast backward in time and the twentieth century vanishes.

Type: Schooner
LOA: 126′10″/38.68m
Beam: 25′5″/7.76m
Draft: 13′11″/4.24m
Displacement: 250 tons
Builder: Camper & Nicholson
Year: 1910
Hull: Wood
Engine: 2 Caterpillar/250 hp each
Speed: 13 knots/ max. speed: 18/19 knots
Sail area: 800 sq m

I am completely open-minded about the superstructure styling but my basic feelings are inclined towards gracefulness, elegance, and soft flowing lines. I believe that a yacht is a feminine creature and her lines and appearance should echo that gender. The other approach, of aggressive paramilitary angular lines, is fine for small high-powered vessels but when applied to larger yacht concepts does not seem appropriate and the design tends to date quickly. My feelings are the same regarding automobile design. I much prefer the body of the "E" type Jaguar to that of the Lamborghini Countach. The "E" type's soft flowing dateless lines designed twenty-five years ago still look elegant whereas the Lamborghini with all its macho lines and angles and aggressive air scoops looks striking but has become tiring to the eye and could never be classed as elegant in the same way as the "E" type could.

There is a trend toward making the main deck area the full width of the hull. I try to keep away from this as it often complicates circulation around the vessel, makes cleaning the windows a nightmare, and means that fenders have to be hung on very long lines from the second deck which never looks particularly shipshape.

Having resolved the main aesthetic and functional aspects of superstructure the other criteria are the detailing of equipment and placement of accessories such as davits, rails, boarding ladders, radar, masts and satellite communication domes, etc. These elements need careful consideration or they can easily spoil the overall profile of the superstructure.

I always approach the interior in two stages, the planning and the decoration. Planning the interior can be a very challenging task due to the restricted available space. Obviously the first consideration is the machinery space, the basic parameter of the hull and allocation of engine ducts, etc. We work in close cooperation with the Naval architects to establish this information, then, with the owners' brief to hand, set about planning the layout.

How the space is distributed is of prime importance. I like to minimize passageways or disguise them by creating a lobby along their length. Passages and stairways should be as wide as possible in order to relieve the problem of claustrophobia. I try to create a greater feeling of space than actually exists and avoid the obvious use of large expanses of mirror in doing so.

Overhead panels of gloss lacquer are my favoured remedy for elevating low ceilings. However, this technique has to be carefully balanced with the other decorative finishes or the result can be rather vulgar and discotequish.

As to the style and decoration of the interior, I try to achieve designs that are successful just for their form and detail, so that if you forget all the colour, it still looks good. It is like the perfect female face, if the bone structure is right, it doesn't need makeup. I try to create the form then apply the makeup in terms of fabrics and colour to suit the client's taste. I never rely on the fabrics to make the room.

It is also important to include items of personality into the decoration, a specially chosen antique or hand-made table lamps, for example. In one instance, we have based the whole salon decoration around a three-hundred-year-old Japanese screen which forms a major focal point and gives the room an individual and personal character.

I try to avoid the built-in "machine look" where the table has the hole for your glass and there is a slot for your magazine. This can appear to be well thought out and "cleverly designed," but people are flexible, they are not robots, and the magazine ends up covering the hole for the glass, which, having lost its place, spills its contents irretrievably in the slot for the magazine! Generally I try to avoid gimmicky gadgets, the hydraulically operated "pop up" television may be a nice idea but it can also have a mind of its own and decide to only "pop up" half way when you least want it to. I try to aim for a more humane and homely approach and try to avoid too much built-in furniture.

On smaller craft, say below 35 metres, or very high speed craft, this aim is not always feasible or appropriate and the built-in look can become necessary due to the restriction of space.

Careful coordination of finishes is essential particularly in confined areas. I try to create an overall harmony throughout the yacht so that it has a feeling of oneness.

Regarding detail elements such as handles, light switches, thermostats, air conditioning outlets, etc., lack of attention to the placing of these items can ruin an otherwise well designed room.

Attention to architectural detail together with our thorough coordination of all the decorative elements can be very time consuming but short cuts cannot be made. The whole is the sum total of its many parts and the more attention that you give to the parts the better is the overall result.

We adopt our design philosophy from the old saying, "It's no good spoiling the ship for a halfpenny worth of tar!"

Terence Disdale

Rio Rita

Rosenkavalier

Type: Motor Yacht
LOA: 217'9"/66.4m
LWL: 178'/54.3m
Tons: 761.57 gross
Designer: Cox & Stevens
Builder: Krupp Germaniawerft Yard,
  Kiel, Germany
Hull: Steel
Year: 1929
Engine: Original Krupp 6 cylinder, 4
  stroke 750 h.p. @ 250 rpm
Speed: 12.5 knots, cruising

Rosenkavalier was originally named *Haida*. She was commissioned by Max Fleischmann to be designed by Cox and Stevens, and was constructed and powered by Krupp at their Germaniawerft Yard at Kiel. The year was 1929, and Fleischmann, whose money seemed immune to the exigencies of recession, spared no expense on the yacht. He was an avid deep-sea fisherman and he used *Haida* to travel to far oceans in pursuit of his sport.

In 1941 Fleischmann sold *Haida* to the United States Navy. She shortly thereafter emerged from the Craig Shipbuilding Company of Long Beach, California, converted from a "Queen of the Sea" to an "Iron Lady" dressed in battleship gray. Reinforced with heavy steel plate, armed, equipped and renamed *USS Argus* for the occasion of war in the Pacific, she plied the southern coast of the United States performing patrol duties.

USS Argus survived the war and was sold in 1948 to Egyptian Maurice Ada, cotton magnate, and close friend of and confidant to King Farouk. Ada took his yacht out of uniform, but did little else in the way of improvements. The yacht stayed in Alexandria until King Farouk was overthrown. Ada left Egypt on his yacht and sailed to the tax haven of Cannes.

The yacht remained in the Mediterranean for some time. Her name was changed to *Sarina* and she again changed owners. She was falling into disrepair until she was bought by Loel Guinness in 1969. Guinness spent a decade rebuilding her and thoroughly renovating her engines. He sold the yacht to Robert Stigwood, the Australian businessman and film producer. *Sarina* then made the rounds of the rich and the famous, traveling to New York, Miami, Mustique, and London. At this time she was equipped with satellite communications and the latest navigational electronics.

In 1981 *Sarina* changed hands again. Renamed *Rosenkavalier*, she became the home away from home of a wealthy recluse and keen sailor. The new owner, sensitive to the history and style of the yacht, redecorated the rooms with the aid of French and Swiss craftsmen. He also serviced all the mechanics of the boat.

A vintage yacht such as *Rosenkavalier* well deserves the attention now afforded to her.

JAMES MORTIMER

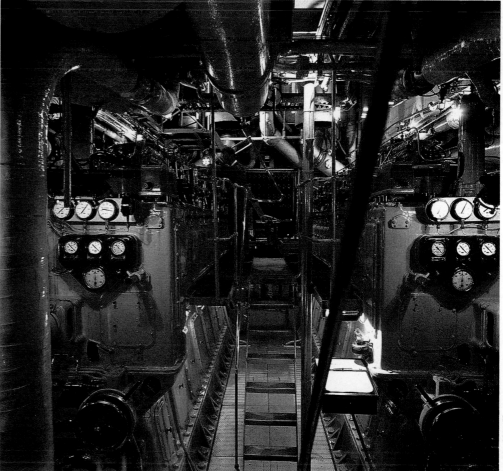

JAMES MORTIMER

Rosenkavalier

Sakara

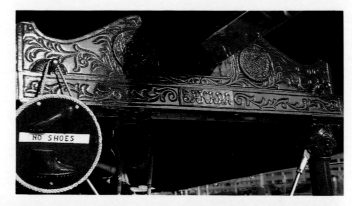

Type: Schooner
LOA: 98′9″/30.10m
Beam: 22′9″/6.93m
Depth: 14′2″/4.26m
Builder: G. Lawley & Son, Neponset, Massachusetts
Sail area: 630 sq. meters
Year: 1913/rebuilt: 1969
Hull: Wood

*S*akara is a traditional schooner built in 1913 by Lawley. She has had a long and rich history and is now owned by the Fayed family of Egypt. She combines old world tradition with an eclectic array of multinational furnishings. The deck salon is a warm room with burgundy tufted leather couches, brocade curtains and an Italian coffee table. Wooden cabinets are panelled in leather. There are interesting and romantic light fixtures and hand carvings everywhere.

The dining salon area is at the base of a steep stairway which has an ornately carved bannister. The settee behind the mahogany table is covered in brown and white pony skin. An original oil painting of *Sakara* dating back to the year she was built is showcased.

The master stateroom is very romantic with sensual deep reds as the dominant hues.

Sakara has a vast deck and beautiful bronze castings with dolphin figures carved into them. Lines are coiled in neat figure eights and the bright work on the cabins is gleaming.

Sakara cruises mostly in the Mediterranean and participates occasionally in the Classic Yacht Regattas that crop up from time to time.

Sequoia

*S*equoia is best known as the U.S. Presidential yacht. She was commissioned as the *USS Sequoia* in early 1933 by President Herbert Hoover and went on to serve eight U.S. presidents. Built in 1925 at the Mathis Shipyard in New Jersey for a Philadelphia family, she was sold to a Texan in 1928 (who coincidently owned Sequoia Oil Company) and was subsequently purchased by the U.S. Department of Commerce for use as a decoy ship to trap rum runners on the Mississippi River. Hoover became enamoured of her and brought her to the Potomac River mostly for fishing and relaxation.

For over forty years, throughout her presidential service, *Sequoia* provided the setting for scores of historic events. Roosevelt planned war and domestic strategy while onboard. Truman held the first conference on nuclear controls and hosted piano parties and occasional poker games on the yacht. Eisenhower made *Sequoia* available to public groups such as wounded Korean War Veterans. In later years, Presidents Kennedy, Johnson, Nixon, and Ford used *Sequoia* for both social and governmental functions. Kennedy had his 46th birthday party onboard, Johnson found her a persuasive setting for promoting his legislative programs with Congress, and Nixon made extensive use of the yacht for his private negotiations with foreign leaders such as Soviet Premier Brezhnev. And it was aboard *Sequoia* that Nixon informed his family of his decision to resign from office. The Ford family enjoyed her for ceremonial and private functions. It was Jimmy Carter who decided to sell her, proclaiming her an unnecessary luxury.

Through the years, 1977-1981, she passed through three owners. In 1981 a Presidential Yacht Trust was created with the intention of preserving her as an historic landmark. *Sequoia* had deteriorated greatly and was in desperate need of attention. It wasn't until 1983 that a concrete program was determined for raising funds in order to renovate her. In 1984 she left her winter quarters in St. Augustine, Florida, to proceed on a six month national "comeback cruise." Captain Giles Kelly helped to map out a route that would take the *Sequoia* from Florida to Texas to New Orleans then up the Mississippi and into the Great Lakes and eventually down the Hudson River to South Street Seaport in New York, then on to the Chesapeake and finally to Washington, D.C. She was met with fanfare and ceremonial hooplah everywhere she went. The fundraising continues for her thorough restoration, with the formal donation of the *Sequoia* to the U.S. Navy planned to coincide with the Statue of Liberty festivities on July 4, 1986.

There are many yachts that are grander than the *Sequoia* but her history gives her special grace and dignity for the American people.

Type: Motor Yacht
LOA: 104'/31.70m
Beam: 18'2"/5.50m
Draft: 4'2"/1.22m
Displacement: 90 tons/full
   displacement: 105 tons
Designer: John A. Trumpy
Builder: Mathis Shipyard, Camden, New Jersey
Year: 1925
Hull: Wood
Engine: Twin Detroit Diesel 671N

ANN STEVENS

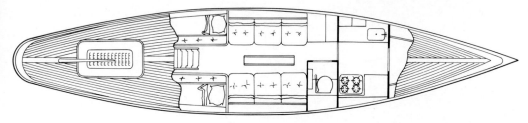

Type: Sloop (fractional rig)
LOA: 45'/13.72m
LWL: 34'6"/10.52m
Beam: 9'7"/2.92m
Draft: 6'/1.83m
Builder/Designer: William Fife, Jr.
Year: 1921
Hull: Wood plank on frame carvel splined
Gross Tons: 14

S heevra is special. There are so many yachts which deserve acclaim and attention. In fact, this whole book is a compilation of very special yachts. However, *Sheevra* is one-of-a-kind. The smallest yacht in our book, she is perhaps the most exquisite. In 1921 a 45-foot racing/cruising sloop was launched at the Fife yard in Fairlie, Scotland. She was christened *Clio*. William Fife was 66 years old at the time and decided she was to be his very own "gentleman's yacht." Three generations at the forefront of yacht design are epitomized in this most personal creation. Her first year in commission she won twelve out of thirteen starts in the restricted under forty-foot waterline class.

The rest of her history is sketchy but it appears there were only three owners between 1926 when Fife sold her and 1983 when she was purchased by Jeffrey Law Olive Adshead, and Donn Costanzo.

The new owners found her in Cannes and brought her to Santo Stephano, Italy to rebuild her. And rebuild her they did! The three young owners had all met while working on the schooner *Puritan*, and were all well versed in yachting. It is their contention that Fife was the best boat builder in the world and their opinion has only been made stronger by their restoration of *Sheevra*. Their story of rebuilding (they did most of the physical work themselves) is truly a case of zen and the art of Fife renovation. Extreme care went into total authenticity. Every bit of salvageable hardware and wood was recycled into the boat. Fittings, lamps, and drawer handles were repaired and now shine as they did years ago.

The accommodations are simple and traditional. A mixture of woods; mahogany, iroco, and cedar are used in the interior. The burgundy tufted velvet settees were lovingly upholstered by Olive. The galley has a beautiful marble slab for rolling dough, a large stainless steel sink, stove, cupboards--everything a real galley would need for an elegant dinner party. The only problem is there is no standing headroom, typical of this type of yacht. You must cook while kneeling!

The owners intend to sail *Sheevra* in many of the Classic Yacht Regattas and Veteran Boat Rallies that come up from year to year in places like Newport, R.I., Porto Cervo, Sardinia, and St. Tropez. They also intend to win.

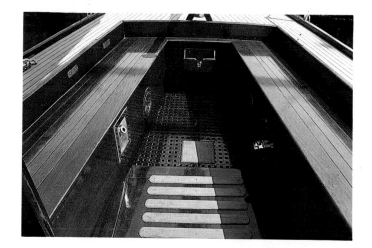

and cockpit. In the back panel of the inboard salon sofa there is an entertainment center facing the dining room from which to enjoy local television or video movies.

The teak and holly sole has been laid athwartship rather than the conventional fore and aft to give the impression of more width. Great attention has also been given to the lighting in the boat vis-a-vis, brass picture lamps, small spotlights, and hidden difused lighting.

The split level layout of salon and dining areas allows two separate groups of people to assemble at the same time.

The cockpit is compact and secure, yet is well designed for daytime and evening lounging. A strong folding dodger protects you from the sun and weather. The cockpit table folds out into four sections or drops its leaves down to shelf size useful for drinks and books.

Shirley B was launched in March 1985, nineteen months from the start of the hull construction. She spent her first five months cruising in the Mediterranean and the Aegean, then made a transatlantic crossing to the Caribbean, and has plans to be in Australia for the America's Cup race.

Shirley B

Shona Boy

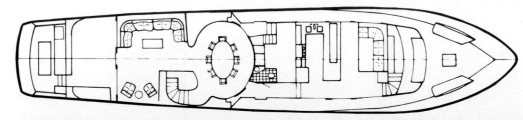

Type: Motor Yacht
LOA: 103'/31.41m
Beam: 21'3"/6.47m
Draft: 5'6."/1.67m
Builder: Broward Marine
Interior Designer: Gertrude Denison
Year: 1985
Hull: Aluminum
Engines: 2 Detroit Diesel 12V92TAM

DONNA AND KEN CHESLER

Shona Boy, a magnificent 103-foot yacht, was created for a company by Broward Marine and Yacht Interiors, of Fort Lauderdale. Now, when top-drawer yachting people gather in Perth, Australia to observe the America's Cup races, they'll have to make room for the American-made *Shona Boy* among their Benettis, Burgers, and Feadships.

The company's representatives visited Broward Marine once a month during the year-long building process to check on progress and to be present for each phase of the custom crafting. They were also involved in the selection of the interior features executed by G. W. Denison of Yacht Interiors.

"Each yacht takes on the personality of the owners," says interior designer, Gertrude W. Denison. "Their objective for this particular vessel was to have a traditional yacht with a somewhat Victorian feeling." The owners' preference for tradition is captured in the rich panelling and cabinetry designed by Tres Converse.

There are special features that make *Shona Boy* one-of-a-kind. For example, the dining salon is constructed in an oval shape with pocket doors that blend with the hand-finished panelling and moldings. The overhead lighting, designed to reflect the shape of the dining table, shines over the inlaid compass rose.

The stylish interior of *Shona Boy* features cheerful and elegant rattan furnishings in the aft deck, beautiful raw silk fabric in the main salon and master stateroom, and a banquette lounge area complete with wine storage behind leaded glass doors in the lower salon. The table in this salon is teak inlay and is just one of the many examples of the fine wood workmanship which is the mainstay throughout this Broward.

DONNA AND KEN CHESLER

DONNA AND KEN CHESLER

Designer's Notes

Designing a yacht interior is much more demanding than designing a home interior—an error or miscalculation of an inch or two on the furnishings can be a costly disaster requiring the incorrect piece to be altered.

That's why precision is such an important part of the design planning stage for my company, Yacht Interiors at Broward Marine. Most furnishings are built-in, and everything from dishes to candlesticks must be secured. The most efficient and effective way to secure each piece of furniture and each accessory is something I have learned over time. Experience has made me familiar with sources for yacht furnishings, too. These include specialized kitchen applicances, water and mildew resistant materials, and custom millworking especially for yachts.

There is also a psychological aspect to designing yachts. Countering the claustrophobia of small spaces, avoiding colors and patterns conducive to sea-sickness and creating a light and airy feel in the lower deck accommodations are skills that must complement the natural good taste of a designer for yachts.

Gertrude Denison

THE BROCHURE PEOPLE, FT. LAUDERDALE, FL.

Type: Motor Yacht with Cockpit
LOA: 104'/31.72m
Beam: 22'/6.71m
Draft: 7'6"/2.29m
Designer: Jack B. Hargrave/Ernest Bonnamy
Builder: G. de Vries Lentsch, Holland and Merrill Stevens of Florida
Year: 1969
Hull: Steel
Engines: Twin Caterpillar D343TA diesels, 6 cylinder 460hp
Speed: 14.5 knots @ 2100 rpm maximum

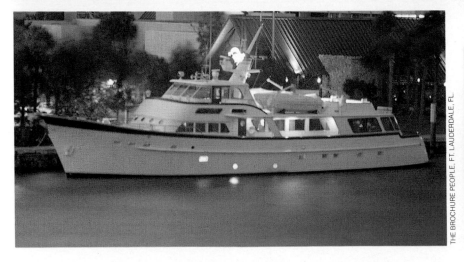

THE BROCHURE PEOPLE, FT. LAUDERDALE, FL.

THE BROCHURE PEOPLE, FT. LAUDERDALE, FL.

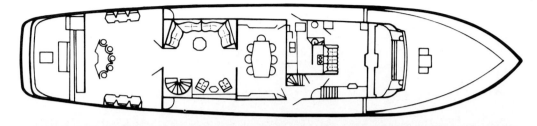

*T*op Secret is a dramatic boat. The interior is like a motion picture set for an Errol Flynn swash-buckling adventure movie. She was designed and created under the supervision of the famous French designer/architect Ernest Bonnamy who was responsi-ble ,for the *Ile de France*, and the Barquentine *Sea Cloud*, Mrs. Horace Dodge's 350-foot *Delphine*, Bar-bara Hutton's London house, and the lobby of the Plaza.

Top Secret is uniquely styled in a mode of Scandi na-vian antiquity reminiscent of the twelfth century Viking era. Her interior, handcrafted from massive ash, oak and teak, is accentuated by 2,000 original draw-ings. The designs are carvings, etchings, sculptures and reliefs, rendered by fourteen artists out of wood, gran-ite, tile, metal, and glass. For example, ash double doors leading from the bar area into the main salon have intri-cately carved ivory pulls on the forward surface. View-ing the closed doors from aft, the leaded stained glass windows depicting Saxon King Harold, a Viking war-rior, are visible, and an inset in the aft lounge bulkhead adjacent to the doors are windows depicting the Viking invasion of Northeastern England in 1066. Within the salon, ash beams project from port to starboard to the center of the overhead. The overhead itself is made up of square panels of Venetian red suede cloth. Each inboard beam end has a unique sculpture of a head facing down. To enumerate all of the designs would be virtually impossible, for everywhere there is another delightful little detail. Every drawer panel is carved, the armrests on the settee are little sculptures, the switch covers are carved, and gargoyles gape at you from vari-ous corners. The walls are irregularly planked in ash fastened by pegs. Bronze plaques cover all the ceiling fixtures. The raised pilothouse access is just forward of the dining salon via a curved stairway. There is an observation lounge with terrific visibility and all of the latest navigational aids. Port and starboard doors lead to a wraparound bridge deck and to the boat deck area.

There are luxurious accommodations for eight and crew's quarters for five. The master suite on the lower level amidships, enjoys the same theme as the rest of the boat. The ceiling is beige suede cloth panels, supported by suede covered strips, studded with brass. Two mas-sive ash beams end in sculptured heads. The bulkheads are pegged ash. From the beams on the portside hangs a canopy striped like a Viking sail with a dark green scal-loped valence inboard. The king- size bed of sculptured ash, lies beneath this. The master bath is panelled in ash with eight individually painted Rocky Mountain quartz inserts which tell a story of Viking warriors returning home with treasure and slave girls to their chieftan. The painting technique here was inspired by the Lascaux Cave paintings.

The starboard guest stateroom has a connecting bath which has a secret door leading from the shower room to the serf's quarters. This hideaway tops off the experi-ence of living a fantasy on board *Top Secret*.

•

Vagabunda

Volador

Type: Ketch-rigged Maxi Cruiser
LOA: 81'/24.70m
LWL: 66'4''/20.20m
Beam: 18'5"/5.6m
Draft: 9'10"/3.0m
Displacement: 42 tons
Designer: German Frers
Interior Designer: Pieter Beeldsnider
Builder: Huisman Shipyard,
  Vollenhave, Holland
Year: 1983
Hull: Aluminum
Engine: Mercedes OM402 V8
  cylinder, 240 hp
Max sail area: 288 sq. meters

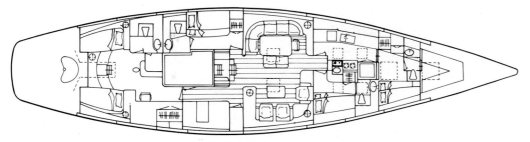

THEO KAMPA

*V*olador is an aluminum luxury ketch rigged Maxi cruiser designed by German Frers and built by the famed Dutch Huisman Shipyard. Masterful engineering has created light-weight construction techniques compatible with an elegant accommodation plan. Foam-cored teak below decks does not forego aesthetics but at the same time this technique developed by Huisman, is up to 40 percent lighter than conventional construction.

For a yacht that is so fast and appears to be so racy, you might imagine that she had to be sailed by a large crew, but this is not the case. The use of electric winches and Huisman designed roller furling on the head sails and mizzen minimize crew requirements. In fact hydraulics do most of the heavy work on the boat including the operation of the ingenious combination boomkin/anchor windlass, dinghy platform swim ladder. Huisman doesn't believe that small vulnerable motors have any business on a cruising boat.

The main salon is comfortably separated into dining and entertaining areas. A leather settee curves around the dining table and a two person love seat is fixed to the centerline of the boat and acts as a kind of divider. The owner of *Volador*, a German industrialist, believes that dining and socializing are two separate activities therefore comfortable armchairs are built-in around a coffee table. The service areas of the boat are both beautiful and efficient. The galley has ample counter space and cabinets designed especially for cups, dishes, glasses. A drawer in the bar pulls out on runners to make it simpler to find the right bottle.

The owners' aft stateroom features two three-quarter size beds with a dressing chair on either side of the companionway. There is also a desk in the owners' cabin which opens into a lady's dressing table. The navigation station boasts a full-size chart table and is replete with Brookes and Gatehouse, SSB, SAT NAV, radar weather fax and more.

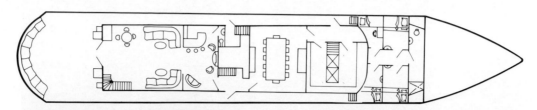

Type: Motor Yacht
LOA: 185′/56.4m
LWL: 167′/51m
Beam: 23′/7m
Displacement: 481.6 tons
Designer: Henry J. Gielow
Builder: Bath Ironworks, Bath, Maine
Year: 1931
Hull: Steel
Engines: 2 V12 Cummings Diesel,
′ 550 hp each

Welsh Princess was originally called *Marguerita*. Her early history had a rather unusual twist. She was commissioned by a Mr. Sorensen, the chauffeur of Henry Ford II. In 1931, the cost of building the yacht was approximately $250,000. Apparently, Mr. Sorensen could not raise the necessary funds and turned to Henry Ford I for assistance. The senior Ford purchased the yacht and gave it to his son Henry Ford II who was only nineteen at that time. *Marguerita* remained in the Ford family for approximately thirteen years. The yacht then changed owners many times. In 1979, she ended up in the Thames River, where she was discovered a few years later by the present owner's son. The boat had several liens against her and therefore was put up for public auction. She was in poor condition and was purchased at a reasonable price by Dragon Yachts, Ltd.; a company which owns five shipyards in the south of England and in Wales, as well as several other yachts of the same vintage as *Welsh Princess*. The yacht was brought to Cardiff, Wales in 1983 to undergo extensive repairs. *Welsh Princess* spent her first season newly rejuvenated in the Mediterranean in 1984.

The boat is now used for charter and has seven private cabins with such names as the Isle of Wight room, Haitian Room, London Cabin, etc. *Welsh Princess* is one of seven vessels, four motor yachts, and three sailboats owned by the Dragon Yachts which include "Welsh" in their names.

The panelling throughout the yacht is the original mahogany and oak. The writing desk dates back to the nineteenth century and there is a vintage, in tune piano. The mirrors and fixtures and the walnut dining table are all from the Ford era, as is the decor in the master stateroom. Ancestral portraits of the Bailey family (Dragon Yachts owners) are hung throughout the main salon and the dining room.

The master stateroom includes his and her bathrooms with old fashioned showerheads that spray from every direction. Window panes are placed over the portholes to give a homey effect.

The main salon is green and beige with select Persian rugs, a game table, a piano and a definitely old world atmosphere. Red leather bar stools and a working fireplace adorn the library. The dining room table is surrounded by striped velvet chairs, original breakfront filigreed in gold and an ornate chandelier.

When the Baileys are on board the yacht, they enjoy events that are a little out of the ordinary. There are photos on the walls depicting a pirate costume party. Another time, they launched a hot air balloon from *Welsh Princess*. Speed boats were sent in pursuit and the balloon landed right on top of one of the boats, causing major confusion.

It seems that *Welsh Princess* was built in 1931 on a whim and today her present owners have a fair sense of whimsy still.

Welsh Princess

Whitefin

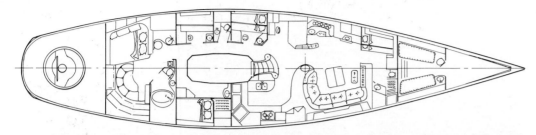

BENJAMIN MENDLOWITZ

*W*hitefin is a magnificent custom-built yacht from stem to stern. She was on the drawing board as soon as *Whitehawk* was sold. Phil Long of Renaissance Yachts conceived both mega-sailboats with California designer Bruce King, and he felt he had learned so much during the construction of the first yacht, that he would set up his own shop, tapping resources from the crew he had previously worked with. To build the new yacht of his dreams, Long constructed a shed over the tennis courts at his house in Camden, Maine and created a backyard boatshop.

Whitefin was designed to be the fastest ocean racing monohull in the world as well as the most aesthetically appealing, and the most seaworthy vessel. Long's original plans were to sail around the world with his sons and a few friends and accumulate trophies in the world's classic offshore races. She is a traditional boat in many ways, not like today's racing machines. She is particularly different in the stern, the slope of the horn timber is steeper than modern racing boats. The racing keel is totally detachable. The flush deck and the sheer line are incredibly graceful. Renaissance Yachts is deeply committed to the notion of a boat as art form. Many different woods went into *Whitefin's* construction including black locust, Pacific yew, end grain balsa, Honduras and African mahogany, Port Orford cedar, and teak.

The interior of *Whitefin*, designed by Joe Artese, is luxuriously comfortable. Her main salon has an elegant flow to it. Woodwork is predominant, and is caressably smooth. She is a family boat—the spacious galley tucked to starboard and adjacent to the companionway allows the cook to enjoy conversation in the main salon. The main salon settee is upholstered in a Scottish wool plaid. The custom ribbon mahogany with yew inlay table can be raised or lowered to coffee table level. It also slides fore and aft and athwartships. A Yamaha organ is built into the forward bulkhead. The skylight, encased in a teak frame dead center above the main salon, is decagonal. Each of the ten pie-shaped panes of bevelled glass are at least 3/4 inches thick. Eye-catching details are everywhere: a beautiful etched glass cabinet to house the crystal, inlaid 'scrimshaw designs, hand-cast bronze sinks, and bronze dolphins. A Rumford fireplace and bookshelves filled with leatherbound volumes give a sensation of being in an exclusive club. All fittings, fixtures, and hardware were chosen with care.

The master stateroom has a queen-size bed, a curved banquette with pillows and a round laminated wooden bathtub.

Whitefin emanates power, strength, and beauty. She is a dream of a determined man, who seems to be always questing. Renaissance Yachts is continuing to build yachts for others who share the dream.

Type: Sloop
LOA: 90′/27.5m
LWL: 71′10″/21.9m
Beam: 21′5″/6.5m
Draft: 9′2″-12′8″/2.74m-3.85m
Displacement: 120,000 lbs.
Designer: Bruce King
Builder: Renaissance Yachts,
Camden, Maine
Year: 1984
Hull: Cold molded wood and WEST
system
Sail Area: 4,050 sq. ft.

JILL BOBROW

BENJAMIN MENDLOWITZ

Whitehawk

Type: Ketch
LOA: 105′/32m
LOD: 92′/28m
LWL: 78′6″/23.9m
Beam: 20′6″/6.2m
Draft: CBU/7′3″/2.21m
　　　　CBD/16′10″/5.12m
Designer: Bruce King
Builder: O. Lie-Nielsen, Maine
Hull: WEST System
Year: 1979
Sail Area: 4,484 sq. ft.

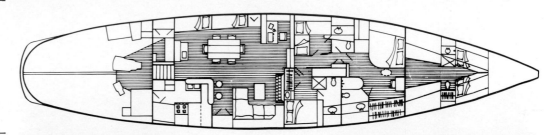

Whitehawk was conceived by Californian Phil Long in 1975, when he commissioned designer Bruce King to design an enlarged version of L. Francis Herreshoff's 72-foot ketch, *Ticonderoga*. Three years later, one of the most spectacular ketches ever built was launched at Lee's Boat Shop in Rockland, Maine, and was sold to a Mr. Zetkov.

Whitehawk's proportions are staggering; her main mast is 116 feet high and there are 4,484 square feet of sail, with the potential of 13,000 square feet. She has a retractable daggerboard that extends to 16 1/2 feet which allows maneuverability and flexibility for entering shallow harbors. Her predecessor, *Ticonderoga*, at one time held thirty world records for speed. *Whitehawk*, at 16 knots under sail has already won several races in New England and in the Caribbean.

Whitehawk is one of the largest hulls ever built using the "WEST System," which stands for "wood epoxy saturation technique." In this process, three diagonal bronze nailed and bonded veneers of cedar were laid over longitudinal mahogany comprising a hull thickness of two and a half inches. The hull's strength is equal to that of a fiberglass hull three inches thick that would weigh from twenty to twenty-five percent more.

The interior is lavishly detailed in a variety of woods including teak, mahogany, and cedar. The main salon is both spacious and cozy. There is a cathedral skylight and a full sized wood burning fireplace framed with Delft tiles. Oriental rugs, brass lanterns and vintage marine art enhance the feeling of warmth and charm.

The master stateroom with queen-size bed boasts a stunning bathtub fabricated from Maine cedar. The cabinets and closets in this room and throughout the boat feature cut away type drawer pulls that provide ventilation—a typical aspect on Herreshoff's yachts.

On deck, there is a tremendous sense of spaciousness. The cockpit is magnificent and comfortably seats twelve. In the center is a dining table with built-in icebox. The helm is a hand-carved teak wheel with a beautiful binnacle and twelve-inch Sestral compass reminiscent of the golden age of yachting. *Whitehawk* is simply a modern classic in every sense of the word.

Xarifa

Xarifa was built in 1927-28 for Mr. Singer (of sewing machine fame). She was constructed as a steamboat at White and Cowes in England, who had a reputation in those days of building the finest steel hulls. *Xarifa* has sailed around the world at least seven times. In 1939 the boat was in Hamburg, when she was confiscated by the Germans and used during the war years to transport coal. After the war she was bought by German scientist, Hans Hass and used as a research vessel. Hass and his wife Lotte, and a group of their colleagues devoted all of their time to biological/philosophical marine research. Similar to Jacques Cousteau, Hass and company traveled to exotic waters for various experiments and underwater discoveries. There are vintage photographs in Hass's book, *To Unplumbed Depths* of *Xarifa* at anchor in the Red Sea and the Barrier Reef. In 1958, the Hass's retired from their sea voyages with *Xarifa* and sold her.

The present owner first encountered her in Singapore. He purchased her in 1960 and has kept her ever since. Having been a work boat for so many years she was due for major renovation to be converted to a yacht. She was delivered first to Antibes from Singapore and then brought to La Spezia to Cantieri Navale Inma to begin her renovation. Everything was removed from her and she was totally gutted. It happened at that time that a cruise ship called the *Liberté* which was formerly the *Bremen* and had been acquired from the Germans after the war was being salvaged and sold. Much of that vessel was taken apart and whole cabins and deck planks were used to reconstruct *Xarifa*. Thus *Xarifa* has a lot of history accumulated within. The main salon has eclectic old world charm and her five cabins accommodate ten people.

Xarifa is strictly a family boat. She is most frequently seen at the dock in Monte Carlo, and she cruises around the Mediterranean each summer. Her name in Egyptian means "beautiful thing" and she certainly lives up to it.

COMPLIMENTS OF CARLO TRAGLIO

TONY MORGAN

Type: Three-masted Schooner
LOA: 155'/47.2m
LOD: 145'/44.2m
Beam: 30'/9m
Draft: 17'/5.2m
Builder: White & Cowes, England
Year: 1928
Hull: Steel
Tonnage: Gross: 275; Net: 165
Engines: Deutz Diesel 230 hp at 600 rpm
Sail area: 5900 sq. ft.

Ristorante

Ristorante

SV 6 10